Politics of Confusion

"When we see men of a contrary character,
we should turn inwards and examine
ourselves."

Confucius
Chinese philosopher & reformer (551 BC - 479 BC)

Nelson Jackson

Defining Politics: Science or Strategy

"Fine words and an insinuating appearance are seldom associated with true virtue."

Confucius

What is the definition of politics?

pol·i·tics

noun*(used with a singular or plural verb)*
the science or art of government.[1]

Arguably politics can be traced back to Aristotle and Plato, where their written contemplations of the subject matter has endured and been emulated in governing manifestos by mostly westernized nations. There are scholars who have sought and still seek to trace the entomology farther back historically to the Mysteries of Egypt and portrayed as a legacy stolen and bastardized to deliberately deny its origins and circumvent the truth. No matter which school of thought you choose to subscribe, politics has placed an indelible hold on our actions and aspirations and defines all of man's accomplishments as he interacts with society. Politics are the precursor of government and is the nucleus which binds institutions to human function. Politics can be restrictive and generally takes credit for allotting freedoms; it can be coercive under the guise of maintaining order, while proselytizing that it seeks to do so for the greater good of society.

---

[1]Dictionary..com....politics

In all of its forms and nuances it is at best nebulous and is more metaphysical than substantive, and therein lies its powers of confusion.

One of the definitions of confusion is to be bewildered, lacking clarity and distinctiveness. By combining the terms of politics and confusion one could scarcely formulate a relationship that can be considered as a science, which is a body of facts or systemic truths arranged in an orderly fashion. Politics is the antithesis of science, being neither orderly or containing consistent truths which can be proven to be absolute. In deed and in fact, it has been proven that the more dynamic in theory and application, the greater the success in obfuscation, which ultimately leads to broader appeal. If mathematics could be used as a comparative political template, then outcomes of political philosophy would be predictable with certainty. Since the beginnings of politics as a recognized social function, politics has created more interpretations than the most abstract piece of art. As mankind evolves technically, the basic elements of man's human processes remain immutable with limitless variations to a common theme. Deeply rooted in the human thought process is the fear of the unknown and when man lacks answers to his existential questions, he commonly relies on unproven beliefs to assuage his anxiety.

Man's inability to define political science opens the door to the formulation of strategies, which borrows from the imprecise to supplant beliefs and aspirations. These strategies inspire motivation to make definitive decisions with only a limited percentage of knowledge employed, yet they have the power to build or destroy nations, send people into war and create opportunities to support human endeavors. Strategic thinking requires vision and to be successful must follow clearly defined guidelines for conceptualization. When the objective strategy is to obfuscate and confuse, then the ultimate goal is to create a false sense of satisfaction that can neither be refuted nor quantified. If the societal order is not destroyed or in the active throes of upheaval and one's personal environ is not uncomfortably disrupted, then a portion of the science of politics has been strategically actualized.

It can be universally agreed that all art is neither pleasing nor aesthetically appealing, but it does share a common genre as being positively or negatively provocative. Politics as an art form is abstract and nuanced as it is metaphysical. If one could say, I have a bucket of politics, then it could be easily recognized as a noun with substance and form, however since its power and existence comes from innuendo and strategic outcomes, it is as easily denied as it is acknowledged. Politics in its nuanced art form can be judged by the means being justified by causation and effect and not just the end.

As a methodology, politics is euphemistically referred to as a science, knowledge a fore thought, complete with planning and prediction, but since the subject matter at play involves human activation and accepted consequences, the likelihood of success is at best random. As a methodology it is a preferred strategy or course of action that presupposes fate. If the predictability of a positive outcome is greater than 50%, then it is the preferred alternative to inaction. A strong component of the methodology is the level of manipulation the subject can exert over the outcome to achieve successful implementation, meaning the result is the somewhere near the original prognostication.

Politics and power are mutually intertwined. The former has greater effect of sustainability if the latter is deliberately judiciously applied. For power to exist it must be exercised. A gun hanging on a wall has no power, whereas a gun in the hands of a person with deliberate aim has the effect of attention, the ability to wound or complete the ultimate sanction. Politics shares a parallel position to power in that it cannot exist in a vacuum. Political acts can be past, present or future tense yet simultaneously be infused as both noun and verb. Aristotle altruistically alluded to political science as a noble cause, used to benefit society by bringing order and stability and providing a framework from which the city-state can function efficiently. As a student of multiple sciences, it seems odd that Aristotle records his applications of politics for lofty and idealistic pursuits, while not quantifying the same degree of effort in the misuses of political application.

One could surmise that Aristotle was exercising his own political power to achieve some goal or agenda which would be eternally interpreted as a positive influence of governance. Perhaps he was establishing his legacy and sought to manipulate the level of acceptability for solidification of his role in political theory development.

In Plato's Politicus titled 'Statesman', the Eleatic Stranger asks the Young Socrates after much debate on the roles of artisans and kings and as to whether they are not the keepers of select knowledge; "Shall we call this art of tending many animals together, the art of managing a herd, or the art of collective management?" It is from that point in the discourse that the stranger and the Young Socrates begin the process of delineating the differences in make-up and anatomy among animals leading to how delineate the differences among men. The ruler being defined as one who possesses divine knowledge on the workings and motivations of men and in so knows what it is the best method to govern these creatures that desperately need to be lead. In the continuing discourse, the two scholars use abstractions to define what is wild versus tame with the implication being of animals and carefully weaves the dialogue to the more specific as pertaining to men. The stranger takes the lead in the discourse by reversing roles of being the questioner and states for agreement that they are talking about "And the political science of which we are in search, is and ever was concerned with tame animals, and is also confined to gregarious animals." Perhaps in part they both come to the same realization that their generalizations do not satisfy the want of definition as to what is political science.

The conclusions can be put in modern terms as; "I might not be able to define it, but I know it when I see it (in operation)."

The preferred answer as to what is political science is deliberately defined imprecisely for academicians and given a brief precise definition for the layman to let him or her according to their level of knowledge draw their own conclusions which generally means being satisfied with the definition. The common expression, "they are playing politics" in making that decision totally negates the possibility that politics is inherent in every decision that impacts two or more people. Therein is the underlying problem with the definitions of politics as a science because if it were to be specific then with each application the equation would be this will yield that immutably and without equivocation.

Is political science a virtuous endeavor or is it the manipulation of the masses by those who possess power through force and coercion or through acquisition by persuasion? Do we acquiesce to power or do we empower people to make the unpleasant decisions from which we admit we have no expertise? Do we collectively agree to allow select persons to regulate us and decimate our monies on programs and policies of our own choosing, or are we lead as sheep and surrender our control of the wages of our labor? Like atomic power its uses can be used for good or evil. Altruistically politics is the glue that binds together the functions of government which begs the questions of the roles of government.

Bricks and mortar can be combined together to make a building, just as people and politics combined together are the underpinnings of an orderly society. When the opposite application is conceived, obstacles are created which serve as stumbling blocks.

Regional Politics

"By nature, men are nearly alike; by practice, they get to be wide apart."

Confucius

In these United States we are a collective group of people from many diverse backgrounds. Enclaves of ethnic populations have retained for decades their cultural perceptions of politics, which to the indigenous group are accepted and traditional, but to the outsider appear disjointed and naive. This diversity in itself is problematic for the political scientist to quantify or qualify and at its best is confusing scientifically. In Plato's Statesman a part of the discourse was to separate species for purposes of clarification into two distinct groups; cloven foot versus hoofed in animals and tame versus wild to the point where the stranger interjects the quality of being garrulous. It was at that point that both Young Socrates and the stranger decide to proceed with caution, because the introduction of speech adds the essential dimension to the defining of what is political science. Language and culture in general contribute to high levels of confusion. The nuances of expression as interpreted based on genealogical biases can be violations of traditional mores.

What is perceived as a weakness in one group are acts of civility to another and acts of strength can be perceived as bullying to still another.

Using language as a yardstick, a linguistic anthropologist may begin in the region of the United States, euphemistically titled 'New England', comprising such states as Rhode Island, Connecticut, New Hampshire, Maine and its unofficial capital, Massachusetts. Looking from a geographical perspective it is easy to surmise the aquatic route of many of the first settlers who were deliberate in their navigation. These early settlers were not the classic explorers who were seeking discovery, but relied on existing data and knowledge of good and habitable environs to extend the British Empire. In essence these were people with a plan. The heavy lifting of exploration had already been borne by the conscripted sailors, exiles and wayfarers who were essentially expendable to failure. The 'new' settlers were educated with skills like engineering, carpentry, animal husbandry and mercantilism. Perhaps the most important skill set the 'new' settlers brought to the "New World' was government. Based on the geographical distance of control that 'Old England' sought to exercise over its North American territorial possession, the first order of business would have been to establish titular heads over these provinces who carried the spirit and letter of English law and custom. In order to communicate clearly to the inhabitants and enunciate the edicts of the parent country, these political mercenaries must understand and be able to articulate those precepts that they were sworn to uphold.

The language of politics would be a hierarchical caste system of sorts; the aristocrats speaking in proper English dialect to the less educated wayfarers who had paved the way and spoke a combination of English with a smattering of native dialect derived from the indigenous people already inhabiting the land.

In order to establish order and set up political foundations, the ability to communicate from top to bottom must be made as seamless as possible. Herein lies the basic nuance of politics as communicated through the lens of language. Intent and vision must remain reserved for the elite, while incorporating the lessor intellectually endowed as willing but unwitting stakeholders in some grand undertaking where they would be beneficiaries. The promise of cheap land was a lucrative inducement in rewarding the converted to blindly follow the politically endowed.

With land would come the assessment of taxes dating back to feudal land ownership, whereas the labor leased the land, they would never truly own it.

As the vision of the 'New World' would begin to materialize, two forces would begin to immediately collide; the increase in population and the methods of governance to manage the vastly scattered citizenry claimed as members of the British Empire. Government structure would have been the easy part, because the British had decades of experience in the methods of colonization. The more complex part would be to cultivate new leadership in the nuance of political suasion uniquely adapted to the changing demographic far removed from its parent body. This experiment was the genesis of regional politics which still exists currently. A multitude of questions would have to be addressed prior to strategy development. First and foremost; what were the aspirations of the people who left everything behind in England to journey to an unknown land with all the mysticism's of the unknown? The common accepted historical explanation was that these were people who launched out seeking religious freedom.

Without qualifying that explanation, but as examined from a political perspective, one could conclude that those given the responsibility of governance would employ a political methodology consistent with the aspirations of the client population, namely freedom from the tyranny of religious persecution. Imagine someone sitting in a big chair back in grand old England with servants at his or her beck and call saying; "let them have their religious wanderlust and heathen worship practices. Bottom line we will have removed them from the orthodox people who worship the Church of England

and want them gone, and let them settle an ocean away where we can tax the hell out them for this freedom." The overall objective would be to sell this freedom at a cost so inconspicuous that the reward will far overshadow the burden.

This is basic Politics 101. Basic carrot and stick with one caveat; persuasion of the recipient that he/she first planted the carrot and therefore has the right to possession.

The second question the erstwhile politician would ask; is how do I communicate colloquially to my client the great selling points of this advantage to worship unencumbered by an overreaching, intrusive government that seeks to limit his civil rights? The thought process may have been to speak in a manner with the voice of the authority of England seasoned with the right measure of treasonous rhetoric to cultivate insurances that the client is in control of his destiny. These are at best arrogant propositions which bears the remnants to this day of language/dialect idiosyncrasies which have caused the residents of 'New England' to be labeled as pseudo-intellectual superior people so disdained by other regions of this country. Example: the pronunciation of car as 'cah' or the word bar as 'bah', direct manifestations of English influence.

This is just a small measure of the confusion of political communication and innuendo of language with subtle emphasis on words and phrases which can completely change the dynamic of intent. Interpretations of the definitions of politics are equally obscure and manner and method of how it is communicated has the potential to obfuscate the most detailed contractual application.

The Mid-Atlantic Region has its own distinctness. Politically this area is known as the de facto power base of the country. The states of New York, Pennsylvania, Delaware, Maryland, New Jersey and the seat of the Nation's Capital, Washington DC are described by detractors and devotees alike as the bastion of liberal thinking, the money mecca of politicism and the mercantile progenitor of western civilization. Its influence spreads to as Far East as the compass can record and is the pulse of the economic anatomy of America. Equally disdained by other regions of the country for reasons unrelated to intellectual elitism, it is the place where the elite go to ply their trade. The member states all have water access and control the commerce of an entire nation with exception only to California on the western shore. Initially this region was settled by less enlightened people than its northern neighbors, but motivated by an industriousness not equaled in the annals of civilization. This region originally looked on the slave trade as a means to an end, which caused its inhabitants to work more shoulder to shoulder with its coerced immigrant populous. The view of having to look a man in the eye was far different than the view from looking out on the porch of a southern plantation. The value of a man was more calculated by his net worth in effort then by his differences in skin color and culture. As a result there was a more amalgamation of cultures which blended to make a unique population.

The ultimate miscegenation of culture, race and gender spawned from the Mid-Atlantic Region. Politics in this region would require experiential exposure and those successful in its application would have to have an unflinching demeanor with little or no apprehension when confronted with immediate identifiable traits. Often as not the average citizen could speak English, eat Chinese food on occasion and dance to Latin music on Friday night. He or she could very easily like southern fried chicken on Sunday, eat crabs or other seafood on Saturday and recite Yiddish homilies while listening to jazz in an Italian bar. This region is and was the great American melting pot, and anyone who chose to exercise politics as a vocation would be required to be well versed in multi-culturalism. Once again the language of politics would have to carefully constructed as apply broad appeal with as little direct reference to specific ethnicities as possible.

If politics can be construed as a science in this venue, then the summation of conclusions would be to maintain as many generalities as possible to not alienate any specific voting bloc and appeal to the broad masses on issues that are common to the whole group. There is no text written, nor standard regulation of conduct which can adequately prepare or shape the personality of persons not specifically endowed with abilities to capture the attention of such a spectrum and sell propositions previously not considered attainable. Therein lays the definition of the art form of politics. Like a musician who is declared a prodigy or an artist gifted with the skill to paint intricate details, there is no quantifiable evidence that politics in its finest applications can be taught to those based on training and study alone. The ability to motivate people, especially those of diverse backgrounds, to rally around a salient project or program is an inexact science at best and if the mandate to achieve a political goal is given to persons not endowed with special dispensation, the end result is confusion, not meeting the standard of political success. Again the definitions of confusion are to be bewildered, lacking clarity and distinctiveness.

The southern region of the country has its own interesting distinction of being a paradox of political application. The science of politics has been demonstrably administered in this region in a judicial manner strictly to suit the needs and aspirations of a population. Agrarian demands far superseded any rational application of equanimity for any order or regulation not in line with its ideology of power, wealth or justice. A cultural anthropologist could ask the question; 'what came first, the bigot or the bigotry'? It seems clear that in terms of necessity where the primary goal was to extract a labor force from somewhere, who would have little or no personal aspiration for wealth, mainly because they wouldn't have a clue as to where they were, a language barrier giving advantage to the dominatrix and preventing little or no family values to be nurtured, then it appears that the bigot and bigotry were hatched simultaneously.

If one would assign religious personification to it, then America had spawned the devil.

From a political perspective, the pre-Civil War and Antebellum South was controlled by an elite few that had acquired immense wealth through land ownership. Whether they were formally educated or had anointed themselves as such, challenges from working classes or small farmers could be easily stifled by the power they wielded through wealth. The adage, money talks and all else walks probably has its entomology in Dixie. Decision making was largely predicated with agrarian interests at the forefront; the American South was a cornucopia of agriculture, both plant and animal, and its ideal growing seasons easily became the breadbasket of the country and as improved methods of transportation became more available, international markets flourished with American produce.

Since the chasm between the educated and the illiterate was so definitive, the controlling class made good uses of its plebian plebiscite population for labor, consumerism and mischief, if so was needed. The airs of the European genteel, though thought to be arrogant and too progressively enlightened, were imitated in costume and behavior, at times with most unflattering humor.
As they say in the land of the blind, the one eyed man is king. With nothing substantial to compare and no time or inclination for post-secondary education, one would have to accept that what was nearest to their environment was worth coveting. If the rich land owner said that emancipation was wrong and even cruel to the Negra, then surely he has the best interest of the south in mind, because he has so much to lose. This reasoning left no room for the lowliest of citizens to consider the long term ramifications of their own plight.

As time moved forward, in some ways the south stayed the same. With its own enunciation of language, its caste system and the commonality of being on the wrong side of history in losing the war, an ideology unique to the region was at much developed as it was maintained.

The resulting political posture was that the people voted monolifically with the main demarcation of ideology being race. Blacks were passively progressive and whites were passively regressive with both sides not willing to radically upset the status quo, but rather were content to plod along in progress like a mule in front of a plow. Geographic considerations probably play a big factor in the perceived laid back attitudes of people residing in the southern latitudes of the country. Hypothetically after a hard day's work in sweltering heat, inordinate attention may have been given to the weather as opposed to critical political thinking, in short at the end of the day, southerners probably just wanted to be left alone.

During Reconstruction after the Civil War, the federal government did seek and pass legislation for a policy that the southern states that had succeeded from the Union would not be allowed to make decisions on voting rights and laws without review from Washington. As a result of its defeat in the war, the south was to be treated like a step child and would or could not be trusted to act fairly without big brother review. It could easily be argued through actuarial verification that the track record of the south and it's deeply held ideology to slavery, which had long since transcended economic expedience, needed to be chaperoned in equitable application of Constitution guarantees.

South Westerner's ideologies were distinctly different in several areas because environmental and agricultural factors shaped their philosophies to fit the circumstances. Originally these areas were inhabited by plains Native-Americans, with vast stretches of open flat land on arid dry soil. Since the amounts of grass per acre to feed cattle or sheep were not as plentiful as in rainy, wet climates, farmers needed large tracts of land for grazing.

What we have termed as Mexican now were people who were made up of a combination of Spanish Conquistadors, native inhabitants and from centuries previously, African explorers, which developed a hearty race of people, with brown and bronze skin and the technical ingenuity of the Aztecs, Mayans and Inca's. Not one to engage in long protracted wars, these indigenous people allowed themselves to be pushed farther and farther south giving way to legendary stories about the Alamo and San Juan Hill.

The interlopers in this case were white adventurers who saw potential in the wide open spaces and saw opportunity for wealth long before the oil wild catters discovered black gold or Texas tea, vast petroleum fields. These people thrived on the philosophy that with hard work, stubbornness to weather the elements and no turning the other cheek to the original owners, south western folk lore was born. There was little need for African slaves, because there was a population of indigenous people already adapted to the region, with excellent knowledge of the properties of the landscape.

Politically these were a people who had honed a set of values intrinsic to the region; God fearing when it was convenient, hard working with a spirit to fight rather than negotiate and an attitude that they were ordained by God to be right about all things. Not always content to remain isolationists, they chummed the regions closest to them to spread the gospel of the southwest, generally finding that people who had never lived there just could not appreciate their logic. In later years they were able to take this south west idealism all the way to Washington, with disastrous results. Like the south, theirs was classic 'us against them' philosophy and they clearly did not want to be confused with the rest of the country.

Party loyalty, historically like the rest of the country, has changed over time. One of the defining moments in history, may have been the reluctant pick of Senator Lyndon Baines Johnson, by candidate Senator John F. Kennedy to be his running mate for President of the

United States. Kennedy a liberal democrat from the liberal state of Massachusetts chose a southern democratic Dixiecrat, Johnson, possibly to cement the party for the future or more pragmatically to win southern voters who were so entrenched in party hypnosis, they failed to see that they were getting played.

Some years after the election and Johnson's total switch from southern conservatism to become one of the most progressive liberals in history, totally pushed the southern camp into the Republican Party. Again political opportunists saw the potential to create a powerful counter force to liberalism from the very party which spawned Lincoln. Little by little they began to gain their voice after 1968, when the country was evolving at such a fast pace, it was easy to alienate people who liked to make decisions while they watched the cotton grow. It was easier to say no then give rational consideration to long term ramifications.

Current Republican ideology is reflective of these times, where issues like climate change, immigration and universal healthcare seem to be conversations that will only take place millenniums in the future.

The western region is unique unto itself, located contiguous to the Pacific Ocean, the states that make up this area share lore of being the final frontier, land of redemption and opportunity. The early settlers migrated from the east with promises of good fortune. When word spread east about how fertile and lush the central valley area was for farming, people sold everything they had and transported entire generations in Conestoga wagons.

Later gold and silver rushes added to west coast fever, fishing was an afterthought until it was discovered that some of the most productive seafood areas lay just miles off shore. Port cities sprang up all along the coast.

Politically, American westerners have been labeled as the land of 'fruits, nuts and flakes', an odd sort of conglomeration of political thinking, ranging from the outlandishly progressive, to ultra-conservatism.

California is the de facto core, where it sheer size has become the breeding ground of multi-cultural liberalism in some geographical pockets and various levels of conservatism on the southern and northern ends of the state. This western state claims the origins of Nixonian and Reaganism while providing residence to and political power to ultra-liberalism of San Francisco and Hollywood.

In some political maps, the states of Oregon, Washington, Idaho, Nevada and Arizona are classified as western or Pacific Western states with no delineating distinct regions like the Pacific Northwest which shares a commonality of politicism and geography unique unto itself.

Central America, more commonly known as the Midwest historically has been stereotyped as a neutral, sort of common good sense values region and acted as a buffer between the two high action coastal populations. Politically this region prides itself as the being the cradle of American values.

American Political Foundations

"The people may be made to follow a path of action, but they may not be made to understand it."

Confucius

We are a nation of people who have adopted laws created by a government modeled under the umbrella of being a Republic. A Republic styled government is defined as:

re·pub·lic
 [ri-**puhb**-lik]
noun
1.a state in which the supreme power rests in the body of citizens entitled to vote and is exercised by representatives chosen directly or indirectly by them.
2.
any body of persons viewed as a commonwealth.
3.
a state in which the head of government is not a monarch or other hereditar
y head of state.[2]

Note the paradox: Constantly we are bombarded by people, educators and government officials who insist that we are a democracy and that is not the complete truth. For the sake of comparison and clarity let's define democracy:

---

[2] "republic." *Dictionary.com Unabridged*. Random House, Inc. 29 Aug. 2013.
<Dictionary.com http://dictionary.reference.com/browse/republic>.

de·moc·ra·cy
 [dih-**mok**-*ruh*-see]
noun, plural **de·moc·ra·cies.**
1.
govern-
ment by the people; a form of government in <u>which</u> the supreme power is v
ested in the people
and exercised directly by them or by their elected agents under a free electo
ral system.
2.
a state having such a form of government: *The United States and Canada a
re democracies.*
3.
a state of society characterized by formal equality of rights and privileges.
4.
political or social equality; <u>democratic</u> spirit.
5.
the common people of a <u>community</u> as distinguished from any privileged cl
ass; the common peoplewith respect to their political power.[3]

Under entry #3 in the definition of democracy we find, "a state of society characterized by formal equality of rights and privileges."[4] And to whom is entrusted with this authority and power to insure these rights and privileges? Pray tell not the same people we allowed to usurp the same from us originally only to now benevolently grant them back! The government giveth and the government taketh away; bless be the name of the government. In the words of a state of society, is a perceived state, a hypnotic state, a drunken state or a coerced state? No man gives up his rights feely and willingly in a sober state of mind.

---

[3] "democracy." *Dictionary.com Unabridged*. Random House, Inc. 29 Aug. 2013.
<Dictionary.com <u>http://dictionary.reference.com/browse/republic</u>>.

[4] Dictionary.com....democracy

"(T)the common <u>people</u> of a <u>community</u> as distinguished from any privileg ed class; the common people with respect to their political power.", entry #5 has set the stage to alert us to the fact that under the democracy there are social classes of people and whereas the rights of the privileged are established, the rights of the common people make up the democracy. All of a sudden it feels like there is some advantage in being common. What exactly is the essence of power wielded by the common people? First how did they obtain it and more importantly; how do they successfully employ it? Is it through the ballot, this democratic process, the one where the privileged are exempt? Paradox or deliberate confusion? Who benefits the most from this democracy and who benefits the least? Has there an independent audit, a referendum quantifying the acceptance level of democracy versus all others or the privileged decides what is best for the rest of us? It's a lot like capitalism; those who benefit most from it decide the fate of those who benefit the least and everyone in between is lulled into believing that they too will someday join the elites.

Under the definition of democracy, entry #4 states 'political or social equality; democratic spirit.' Since we are seeking to understand and analyze the precise meaning of politics we can shelve that portion of the entry for the moment, but we do have a fairly strong concept of what social equality means and to date no known democracy has ever lived up to those precepts. In fact one could argue that democracy which is fundamentally majority rule and the will of the people presupposes social equality in that there will always be cases where some will get equal treatment and others will be marginalized. Perhaps this part of the definition should be stated as the right to social equality. The portion of entry #4 citing 'democratic spirit,' is totally ambiguous and suggests that we know what democracy consists of, how it operates and as to whether the recipients consider democracy a good, bad, just or unjust thing.

The two definitions are antithetical to each other, yet at the same time mutually exclusive to each other.

In the Republic, a supreme power is referenced as the titular *head resting in the citizens entitled to vote* and representatives are chosen to exercise the will of the people through this enfranchisement. In the Democracy definition, the government is by the people, where the supreme power is vested *in* the people and *exercised directly* by them. The legal nuances in these two definitions are so voluminous as to be able to keep Constitutional lawyers busy well into future millenniums should they so choose to challenge them. Before we go any further, let us concede that at best this is a democratic republic formed government, designed to confuse the less educated and to favor the elite.

First off, if you accept the republic definition as absolute, than you have sanctioned the historical beginning with the founding fathers, the right to vote was predicated with land ownership, white male citizenry and social status. As a consequence, originally women, blacks, economically challenged or Jimmy the hobo had no legal standing to vote. Representations for these classes were not even a consideration, even though taxes could be levied on them and their labor. Not to marginalize the existence of the thousands of Native-Americans who had inhabited this land centuries before the white man. This republic styled government was designed from the foundations of European feudal law, where the original intent was to accept governance from a king or a lord whom not only exercised control of the land but to include in or on it, people, chattel of all kinds down to the air that was being breathed. European white males recognizing the tyranny of this situation rebelled and insisted on inclusion in the process to determine the rights by which they would be governed. This was in no way a magnanimous gesture for the equality for all citizenry, but self-interest was the engine of this movement. The Roman Empire was exponentially more enlightened than this group of anarchists, because they did include anyone who swore allegiance to the Empire.

Let's not give them a complete pass, because women were not enfranchised, though their status may be arguably equal to or better than feudal Europe. Depending on the social stratum where a woman found herself, she may have had the ability to ascend to high levels of the societal order and may have been able to exercise unequivocal power in the decision making and the directions of societal policy. Captured and defeated colonies could be inculcated into the Roman system, granted without much direct power, but the right to petition the government was fundamental in the Empire.

Philosophy of governance throughout western society is an interpretation and application of the Greek philosophy, primarily that of Plato and Aristotle. The republic type of governance was an attempt to bring reason and order to a standard for application so that societies could have a model for the maintenance of order and all of the other guarantees of liberty promulgated. These theories work well if gone unchallenged or if those involved in scholarly pursuits decide not to look behind the curtain. In analysis of each line in the definition glaring inconsistencies will be revealed, first and foremost how come in explanations of whom and what type of government we have, no two people seem to provide the same answer. One could argue that this is what Plato and Aristotle had in mind when laid down these foundations, but as a student of philosophy, I would argue that these premises were promulgated as a starting point for discussion and debate, not the definitive answer. However, why tamper with something when it is so universally accepted with the masses blindly signing on without question; sort of like the Bible! From this short and concise definition all sorts of mischief can be created.

We are constantly besieged with phrases like original intent, the Founders intent, strict constructivism and legions of interpretations of insight into the true and moral intentions of 40 white males who had been self and electively ordained as the intelligentsia of this New World.

Now think about it; when you hear people talk about original intent, do you honestly believe that even under the most benevolent motives of the founders that they had anyone other than themselves or the people who looked like them in mind. If you do, I'll pay you double for whatever you've been smoking, because even with a bare minimum of knowledge, one would have to concede that these 40 men would have had to have been morally superior to Jesus Christ. If you still can't shake them off their pedestal, all 27 amendments aside, delve into the personal lives of these men as a standard of measurement used to judge almost all of us, called character, and if you don't discover any flaws, I will concede my critique.

Let's examine a few of the most notable:

Thomas Jefferson – owned slaves, dissed Sallie Hemming, oops by the way, he did not sign the Constitution, he signed the Declaration of Independence.
(This is a good question to ask at a dinner party, 98% of your guests will get it wrong.)

Alexander Hamilton – called the Nation's Banker as the founder of the nation's financial system (that's enough to draw and quarter him right there), born out of wedlock in the West Indies (we called that a bastard child), he attended then King's College in New York, later to become Columbia University (attended college is a euphemism for, "did not graduate"), another oops, Hamilton was strong supporter for a strong central government, had an extra-marital affair that caused him to resign as Secretary of Treasury....(the list goes on and on, don't get me wrong, I kinda like the guy, but walking on water…? I doubt it!)

James Madison Jr. – started out as proponent of a strong central government, later shifted to a state's rights advocate, either way to put it mildly he had issues.

Madison and Jefferson originally formed a political party called the Republicans documented to have been argued by historians as the Democratic-Republican Party (the plot thickens, these two guys were no dummies and even though they suspected that in the future most people would be too dumb to do the research, nevertheless these two hedged their bets), after leading the nation into war (1812) and realizing that the country didn't have the power or the present capability to finance a war, this after having dissed his former friend and ally, Alexander Hamilton(the money man), then he decides that a strong central government is not such a bad thing. (he's still one of my favorites because he recognized that there is a certain amount of tyranny in majority rule), he owned slaves and cultivated tobacco, well bless his little heart, he was human and profited off of man's vices, do tell...............!

Now take a look into the lives of the other 38 and send me a note if you find one worth for canonization. I'll make a double dare; go to a cocktail party with some of your most learned friends and ask them to name the signators of the Constitution; you would have a better chance of winning a Chinese lottery then losing this bet!

This is a book about confusion in politics, ask yourself; why wasn't I taught all of this in high school and if I was, then how did I let myself be bamboozled by a bunch of politicians who throw out a bunch of false sound bites and I lap it up like an alcoholic to a drink; just can't help myself! Politicians rely on your lack of knowledge and curiosity, but here's a little tip; most of them can't tell you the difference between a Republic and a Democracy either.

Paradoxes of the American Constitution

"To go beyond is as wrong as to fall short."

Confucius

THE U.S. NATIONAL ARCHIVES & RECORDS ADMINISTRATION

www.archives.gov

S

The Constitution of the United States: A Transcription

Note: *The following text is a transcription of the Constitution in its **original** form.*
Items that are hyperlinked have since been amended or superseded.

We the People of the United States, in Order to form a more perfect Union, establish Justice, insure domestic Tranquility, provide for the common defence, promote the general Welfare, and secure the Blessings of Liberty to ourselves and our Posterity, do ordain and establish this Constitution for the United States of America.

Article. I.

Section. 1.

All legislative Powers herein granted shall be vested in a Congress of the United States, which shall consist of a Senate and House of Representatives.

Section. 2.

The House of Representatives shall be composed of Members chosen every second Year by the People of the several States, and the Electors in each State shall have the Qualifications requisite for Electors of the most numerous Branch of the State Legislature.

No Person shall be a Representative who shall not have attained to the Age of twenty five Years, and been seven Years a Citizen of the United States, and who shall not, when elected, be an Inhabitant of that State in which he shall be chosen.

Representatives and direct Taxes shall be apportioned among the several States which may be included within this Union, according to their respective Numbers, which shall be determined by adding to the whole Number of free Persons, including those bound to Service for a Term of Years, and excluding Indians not taxed, three fifths of all other Persons. The actual Enumeration shall be made within three Years after the first Meeting of the Congress of the United States, and within every subsequent Term of ten Years, in such Manner as they shall by Law direct. The Number of Representatives shall not exceed one for every thirty Thousand, but each State shall have at Least one Representative; and until such enumeration shall be made, the State of New Hampshire shall be entitled to chuse three, Massachusetts eight, Rhode-Island and Providence Plantations one, Connecticut five, New-York six, New Jersey four, Pennsylvania eight, Delaware one, Maryland six, Virginia ten, North Carolina five, South Carolina five, and Georgia three.

When vacancies happen in the Representation from any State, the Executive Authority thereof shall issue Writs of Election to fill such Vacancies.

The House of Representatives shall chuse their Speaker and other Officers; and shall have the sole Power of Impeachment.

Section. 3.

The Senate of the United States shall be composed of two Senators from each State, chosen by the Legislature thereof for six Years; and each Senator shall have one Vote.

Immediately after they shall be assembled in Consequence of the first Election, they shall be divided as equally as may be into three Classes. The Seats of the Senators of the first Class shall be vacated at the Expiration of the second Year, of the second Class at the Expiration of the fourth Year, and of the third Class at the Expiration of the sixth Year, so that one third may be chosen every second Year; and if Vacancies happen by Resignation, or otherwise, during the Recess of the Legislature of any State, the Executive thereof may make temporary Appointments until the next Meeting of the Legislature, which shall then fill such Vacancies.

No Person shall be a Senator who shall not have attained to the Age of thirty Years, and been nine Years a Citizen of the United States, and who shall not, when elected, be an

Inhabitant of that State for which he shall be chosen.

The Vice President of the United States shall be President of the Senate, but shall have no Vote, unless they be equally divided.

The Senate shall chuse their other Officers, and also a President pro tempore, in the Absence of the Vice President, or when he shall exercise the Office of President of the United States.

The Senate shall have the sole Power to try all Impeachments. When sitting for that Purpose, they shall be on Oath or Affirmation. When the President of the United States is tried, the Chief Justice shall preside: And no Person shall be convicted without the Concurrence of two thirds of the Members present.

Judgment in Cases of Impeachment shall not extend further than to removal from Office, and disqualification to hold and enjoy any Office of honor, Trust or Profit under the United States: but the Party convicted shall nevertheless be liable and subject to Indictment, Trial, Judgment and Punishment, according to Law.

Section. 4.

The Times, Places and Manner of holding Elections for Senators and Representatives, shall be prescribed in each State by the Legislature thereof; but the Congress may at any time by Law make or alter such Regulations, except as to the Places of chusing Senators.

The Congress shall assemble at least once in every Year, and such Meeting shall <u>be on the first Monday in December</u>, unless they shall by Law appoint a different Day.

Section. 5.

Each House shall be the Judge of the Elections, Returns and Qualifications of its own Members, and a Majority of each shall constitute a Quorum to do Business; but a smaller Number may adjourn from day to day, and may be authorized to compel the Attendance of absent Members, in such Manner, and under such Penalties as each House may provide.

Each House may determine the Rules of its Proceedings, punish its Members for disorderly Behaviour, and, with the Concurrence of two thirds, expel a Member.

Each House shall keep a Journal of its Proceedings, and from time to time publish the same, excepting such Parts as may in their Judgment require Secrecy; and the Yeas and Nays of the Members of either House on any question shall, at the Desire of one fifth of those Present, be entered on the Journal.

Neither House, during the Session of Congress, shall, without the Consent of the other, adjourn for more than three days, nor to any other Place than that in which the two Houses shall be sitting.

Section. 6.

The Senators and Representatives shall receive a Compensation for their Services, to be ascertained by Law, and paid out of the Treasury of the United States. They shall in all Cases, except Treason, Felony and Breach of the Peace, be privileged from Arrest during their Attendance at the Session of their respective Houses, and in going to and returning from the same; and for any Speech or Debate in either House, they shall not be questioned in any other Place.

No Senator or Representative shall, during the Time for which he was elected, be appointed to any civil Office under the Authority of the United States, which shall have been created, or the Emoluments whereof shall have been encreased during such time; and no Person holding any Office under the United States, shall be a Member of either House during his Continuance in Office.

Section. 7.

All Bills for raising Revenue shall originate in the House of Representatives; but the Senate may propose or concur with Amendments as on other Bills.

Every Bill which shall have passed the House of Representatives and the Senate, shall, before it become a Law, be presented to the President of the United States: If he approve he shall sign it, but if not he shall return it, with his Objections to that House in which it shall have originated, who shall enter the Objections at large on their Journal, and proceed to reconsider it. If after such Reconsideration two thirds of that House shall agree to pass the Bill, it shall be sent, together with the Objections, to the other House, by which it shall likewise be reconsidered, and if approved by two thirds of that House, it shall become a Law. But in all such Cases the Votes of both Houses shall be determined by yeas and Nays, and the Names of the Persons voting for and against the Bill shall be entered on the Journal of each House respectively. If any Bill shall not be returned by the President within ten Days (Sundays excepted) after it shall have been presented to him, the Same shall be a Law, in like Manner as if he had signed it, unless the Congress by their Adjournment prevent its Return, in which Case it shall not be a Law.

Every Order, Resolution, or Vote to which the Concurrence of the Senate and House of Representatives may be necessary (except on a question of Adjournment) shall be presented to the President of the United States; and before the Same shall take Effect, shall be approved by him, or being disapproved by him, shall be repassed by two thirds of the Senate and House of Representatives, according to the Rules and Limitations prescribed in the Case of a Bill.

Section. 8.

The Congress shall have Power To lay and collect Taxes, Duties, Imposts and Excises, to pay the Debts and provide for the common Defence and general Welfare of the United States; but all Duties, Imposts and Excises shall be uniform throughout the United States;

To borrow Money on the credit of the United States;

To regulate Commerce with foreign Nations, and among the several States, and with the Indian Tribes;

To establish an uniform Rule of Naturalization, and uniform Laws on the subject of Bankruptcies throughout the United States;

To coin Money, regulate the Value thereof, and of foreign Coin, and fix the Standard of Weights and Measures;

To provide for the Punishment of counterfeiting the Securities and current Coin of the United States;

To establish Post Offices and post Roads;

To promote the Progress of Science and useful Arts, by securing for limited Times to Authors and Inventors the exclusive Right to their respective Writings and Discoveries;

To constitute Tribunals inferior to the supreme Court;

To define and punish Piracies and Felonies committed on the high Seas, and Offences against the Law of Nations;

To declare War, grant Letters of Marque and Reprisal, and make Rules concerning Captures on Land and Water;

To raise and support Armies, but no Appropriation of Money to that Use shall be for a longer Term than two Years;

To provide and maintain a Navy;

To make Rules for the Government and Regulation of the land and naval Forces;

To provide for calling forth the Militia to execute the Laws of the Union, suppress Insurrections and repel Invasions;

To provide for organizing, arming, and disciplining, the Militia, and for governing such Part of them as may be employed in the Service of the United States, reserving to the States respectively, the Appointment of the Officers, and the Authority of training the Militia according to the discipline prescribed by Congress;

To exercise exclusive Legislation in all Cases whatsoever, over such District (not exceeding ten Miles square) as may, by Cession of particular States, and the Acceptance of Congress, become the Seat of the Government of the United States, and to exercise like Authority over all Places purchased by the Consent of the Legislature of the State in which the Same shall be, for the Erection of Forts, Magazines, Arsenals, dock-Yards, and other needful Buildings;--And

To make all Laws which shall be necessary and proper for carrying into Execution the foregoing Powers, and all other Powers vested by this Constitution in the Government of the United States, or in any Department or Officer thereof.

Section. 9.

The Migration or Importation of such Persons as any of the States now existing shall think proper to admit, shall not be prohibited by the Congress prior to the Year one thousand eight hundred and eight, but a Tax or duty may be imposed on such Importation, not exceeding ten dollars for each Person.

The Privilege of the Writ of Habeas Corpus shall not be suspended, unless when in Cases of Rebellion or Invasion the public Safety may require it.

No Bill of Attainder or ex post facto Law shall be passed.

No Capitation, or other direct, Tax shall be laid, <u>unless in Proportion to the Census or enumeration herein before directed to be taken</u>.

No Tax or Duty shall be laid on Articles exported from any State.

No Preference shall be given by any Regulation of Commerce or Revenue to the Ports of one State over those of another; nor shall Vessels bound to, or from, one State, be obliged to enter, clear, or pay Duties in another.

No Money shall be drawn from the Treasury, but in Consequence of Appropriations made by Law; and a regular Statement and Account of the Receipts and Expenditures of all public Money shall be published from time to time.

No Title of Nobility shall be granted by the United States: And no Person holding any Office of Profit or Trust under them, shall, without the Consent of the Congress, accept of any present, Emolument, Office, or Title, of any kind whatever, from any King, Prince, or foreign State.

Section. 10.

No State shall enter into any Treaty, Alliance, or Confederation; grant Letters of Marque and Reprisal; coin Money; emit Bills of Credit; make any Thing but gold and silver Coin a Tender in Payment of Debts; pass any Bill of Attainder, ex post facto Law, or Law impairing the Obligation of Contracts, or grant any Title of Nobility.

No State shall, without the Consent of the Congress, lay any Imposts or Duties on Imports or Exports, except what may be absolutely necessary for executing it's inspection Laws: and the net Produce of all Duties and Imposts, laid by any State on Imports or Exports, shall be for the Use of the Treasury of the United States; and all such Laws shall be subject to the Revision and Controul of the Congress.

No State shall, without the Consent of Congress, lay any Duty of Tonnage, keep Troops, or Ships of War in time of Peace, enter into any Agreement or Compact with another State, or with a foreign Power, or engage in War, unless actually invaded, or in such imminent Danger as will not admit of delay.

Article. II.

Section. 1.

The executive Power shall be vested in a President of the United States of America. He shall hold his Office during the Term of four Years, and, together with the Vice President, chosen for the same Term, be elected, as follows:

Each State shall appoint, in such Manner as the Legislature thereof may direct, a Number of Electors, equal to the whole Number of Senators and Representatives to which the State may be entitled in the Congress: but no Senator or Representative, or Person holding an Office of Trust or Profit under the United States, shall be appointed an Elector.

The Electors shall meet in their respective States, and vote by Ballot for two Persons, of whom one at least shall not be an Inhabitant of the same State with themselves. And they shall make a List of all the Persons voted for, and of the Number of Votes for each; which List they shall sign and certify, and transmit sealed to the Seat of the Government of the

United States, directed to the President of the Senate. The President of the Senate shall, in the Presence of the Senate and House of Representatives, open all the Certificates, and the Votes shall then be counted. The Person having the greatest Number of Votes shall be the President, if such Number be a Majority of the whole Number of Electors appointed; and if there be more than one who have such Majority, and have an equal Number of Votes, then the House of Representatives shall immediately chuse by Ballot one of them for President; and if no Person have a Majority, then from the five highest on the List the said House shall in like Manner chuse the President. But in chusing the President, the Votes shall be taken by States, the Representation from each State having one Vote; A quorum for this purpose shall consist of a Member or Members from two thirds of the States, and a Majority of all the States shall be necessary to a Choice. In every Case, after the Choice of the President, the Person having the greatest Number of Votes of the Electors shall be the Vice President. But if there should remain two or more who have equal Votes, the Senate shall chuse from them by Ballot the Vice President.

The Congress may determine the Time of chusing the Electors, and the Day on which they shall give their Votes; which Day shall be the same throughout the United States.

No Person except a natural born Citizen, or a Citizen of the United States, at the time of the Adoption of this Constitution, shall be eligible to the Office of President; neither shall any Person be eligible to that Office who shall not have attained to the Age of thirty five Years, and been fourteen Years a Resident within the United States.

In Case of the Removal of the President from Office, or of his Death, Resignation, or Inability to discharge the Powers and Duties of the said Office, the Same shall devolve on the Vice President, and the Congress may by Law provide for the Case of Removal, Death, Resignation or Inability, both of the President and Vice President, declaring what Officer shall then act as President, and such Officer shall act accordingly, until the Disability be removed, or a President shall be elected.

The President shall, at stated Times, receive for his Services, a Compensation, which shall neither be increased nor diminished during the Period for which he shall have been elected, and he shall not receive within that Period any other Emolument from the United States, or any of them.

Before he enter on the Execution of his Office, he shall take the following Oath or Affirmation:--"I do solemnly swear (or affirm) that I will faithfully execute the Office of President of the United States, and will to the best of my Ability, preserve, protect and defend the Constitution of the United States."

Section. 2.

The President shall be Commander in Chief of the Army and Navy of the United States, and of the Militia of the several States, when called into the actual Service of the United States; he may require the Opinion, in writing, of the principal Officer in each of the executive Departments, upon any Subject relating to the Duties of their respective Offices, and he shall have Power to grant Reprieves and Pardons for Offences against the United States, except in Cases of Impeachment.

He shall have Power, by and with the Advice and Consent of the Senate, to make Treaties, provided two thirds of the Senators present concur; and he shall nominate, and by and with the Advice and Consent of the Senate, shall appoint Ambassadors, other public Ministers and Consuls, Judges of the supreme Court, and all other Officers of the United States, whose Appointments are not herein otherwise provided for, and which shall be established by Law: but the Congress may by Law vest the Appointment of such inferior Officers, as they think proper, in the President alone, in the Courts of Law, or in the Heads of Departments.

The President shall have Power to fill up all Vacancies that may happen during the Recess of the Senate, by granting Commissions which shall expire at the End of their next Session.

Section. 3.

He shall from time to time give to the Congress Information of the State of the Union, and recommend to their Consideration such Measures as he shall judge necessary and expedient; he may, on extraordinary Occasions, convene both Houses, or either of them, and in Case of Disagreement between them, with Respect to the Time of Adjournment, he may adjourn them to such Time as he shall think proper; he shall receive Ambassadors and other public Ministers; he shall take Care that the Laws be faithfully executed, and shall Commission all the Officers of the United States.

Section. 4.

The President, Vice President and all civil Officers of the United States, shall be removed from Office on Impeachment for, and Conviction of, Treason, Bribery, or other high Crimes and Misdemeanors.

Article III.

Section. 1.

The judicial Power of the United States shall be vested in one supreme Court, and in such inferior Courts as the Congress may from time to time ordain and establish. The Judges, both of the supreme and inferior Courts, shall hold their Offices during good Behaviour, and shall, at stated Times, receive for their Services a Compensation, which shall not be diminished during their Continuance in Office.

Section. 2.

The judicial Power shall extend to all Cases, in Law and Equity, arising under this Constitution, the Laws of the United States, and Treaties made, or which shall be made, under their Authority;--to all Cases affecting Ambassadors, other public Ministers and Consuls;--to all Cases of admiralty and maritime Jurisdiction;--to Controversies to which the United States shall be a Party;--to Controversies between two or more States;-- between a State and Citizens of another State,--between Citizens of different States,--between Citizens of the same State claiming Lands under Grants of different States, and between a State, or the Citizens thereof, and foreign States, Citizens or Subjects.

In all Cases affecting Ambassadors, other public Ministers and Consuls, and those in which a State shall be Party, the supreme Court shall have original Jurisdiction. In all the other Cases before mentioned, the supreme Court shall have appellate Jurisdiction, both as to Law and Fact, with such Exceptions, and under such Regulations as the Congress shall make.

The Trial of all Crimes, except in Cases of Impeachment, shall be by Jury; and such Trial shall be held in the State where the said Crimes shall have been committed; but when not committed within any State, the Trial shall be at such Place or Places as the Congress may by Law have directed.

Section. 3.

Treason against the United States, shall consist only in levying War against them, or in adhering to their Enemies, giving them Aid and Comfort. No Person shall be convicted of Treason unless on the Testimony of two Witnesses to the same overt Act, or on Confession in open Court.

The Congress shall have Power to declare the Punishment of Treason, but no Attainder of Treason shall work Corruption of Blood, or Forfeiture except during the Life of the Person attainted.

Article. IV.

Section. 1.

Full Faith and Credit shall be given in each State to the public Acts, Records, and judicial Proceedings of every other State. And the Congress may by general Laws prescribe the Manner in which such Acts, Records and Proceedings shall be proved, and the Effect thereof.

Section. 2.

The Citizens of each State shall be entitled to all Privileges and Immunities of Citizens in the several States.

A Person charged in any State with Treason, Felony, or other Crime, who shall flee from Justice, and be found in another State, shall on Demand of the executive Authority of the State from which he fled, be delivered up, to be removed to the State having Jurisdiction of the Crime.

No Person held to Service or Labour in one State, under the Laws thereof, escaping into another, shall, in Consequence of any Law or Regulation therein, be discharged from such Service or Labour, but shall be delivered up on Claim of the Party to whom such Service or Labour may be due.

Section. 3.

New States may be admitted by the Congress into this Union; but no new State shall be formed or erected within the Jurisdiction of any other State; nor any State be formed by the Junction of two or more States, or Parts of States, without the Consent of the Legislatures of the States concerned as well as of the Congress.

The Congress shall have Power to dispose of and make all needful Rules and Regulations respecting the Territory or other Property belonging to the United States; and nothing in this Constitution shall be so construed as to Prejudice any Claims of the United States, or of any particular State.

Section. 4.

The United States shall guarantee to every State in this Union a Republican Form of Government, and shall protect each of them against Invasion; and on Application of the Legislature, or of the Executive (when the Legislature cannot be convened), against domestic Violence.

Article. V.

The Congress, whenever two thirds of both Houses shall deem it necessary, shall propose Amendments to this Constitution, or, on the Application of the Legislatures of two thirds of the several States, shall call a Convention for proposing Amendments, which, in either Case, shall be valid to all Intents and Purposes, as Part of this Constitution, when ratified by the Legislatures of three fourths of the several States, or by Conventions in three fourths thereof, as the one or the other Mode of Ratification may be proposed by the Congress; Provided that no Amendment which may be made prior to the Year One thousand eight hundred and eight shall in any Manner affect the first and fourth Clauses in the Ninth Section of the first Article; and that no State, without its Consent, shall be deprived of its equal Suffrage in the Senate.

Article. VI.

All Debts contracted and Engagements entered into, before the Adoption of this Constitution, shall be as valid against the United States under this Constitution, as under the Confederation.

This Constitution, and the Laws of the United States which shall be made in Pursuance thereof; and all Treaties made, or which shall be made, under the Authority of the United States, shall be the supreme Law of the Land; and the Judges in every State shall be bound thereby, any Thing in the Constitution or Laws of any State to the Contrary notwithstanding.

The Senators and Representatives before mentioned, and the Members of the several State Legislatures, and all executive and judicial Officers, both of the United States and of the several States, shall be bound by Oath or Affirmation, to support this Constitution; but no religious Test shall ever be required as a Qualification to any Office or public Trust under the United States.

Article. VII.

The Ratification of the Conventions of nine States, shall be sufficient for the Establishment of this Constitution between the States so ratifying the Same.

The Word, "the," being interlined between the seventh and eighth Lines of the first Page, the Word "Thirty" being partly written on an Erazure in the fifteenth Line of the first Page, The Words "is tried" being interlined between the thirty second and thirty third Lines of the first Page and the Word "the" being interlined between the forty third and forty fourth Lines of the second Page.

Attest William Jackson Secretary

done in Convention by the Unanimous Consent of the States present the Seventeenth Day of September in the Year of our Lord one thousand seven hundred and Eighty seven and of the Independance of the United States of America the Twelfth In witness whereof We have hereunto subscribed our Names,

G°. Washington
Presidt and deputy from Virginia

Delaware
Geo: Read
Gunning Bedford jun
John Dickinson
Richard Bassett
Jaco: Broom

Maryland
James McHenry
Dan of St Thos. Jenifer
Danl. Carroll

Virginia
John Blair
James Madison Jr.

North Carolina
Wm. Blount
Richd. Dobbs Spaight
Hu Williamson

South Carolina
J. Rutledge
Charles Cotesworth Pinckney
Charles Pinckney
Pierce Butler

Georgia
William Few
Abr Baldwin

New Hampshire
John Langdon
Nicholas Gilman

Massachusetts
Nathaniel Gorham

Rufus King

Connecticut
Wm. Saml. Johnson
Roger Sherman

New York
Alexander Hamilton

New Jersey
Wil: Livingston
David Brearley
Wm. Paterson
Jona: Dayton

Pennsylvania
B Franklin
Thomas Mifflin
Robt. Morris
Geo. Clymer
Thos. FitzSimons
Jared Ingersoll
James Wilson
Gouv Morris[5]

5

Page URL: http://www.archives.gov/exhibits/charters/constitution_transcript.html

U.S. National Archives & Records Administration
8601 Adelphi Road, College Park, MD, 20740-6001, • 1-86-NARA-NARA • 1-866-272-6272

There was no hesitation on my part for including the complete text of the Constitution in this chapter. Perhaps it is one of the most miss-quoted documents of law and history, with its only exception the Bible that has ever been written. It is easy to identify the most pompous and academically challenged individual and groups when they attempt to use the American Constitution as a reference, usually to show how erudite they are and how difficult they will be to fool. Just like when I hear someone say that they are a Christian unsolicited; when someone says that they are evoking the laws of the Constitution, I know that we are in for an avalanche of subterfuge and misinterpretation. Generally these things are taken out of context, deliberately or under the spell of some self-perceived divine revelation that was dispensed to them specifically.

Granted in Ephesians 6 Chapter, Verses 11-13, the Bible says to: "[11] Put on the whole armor of God, that you may be able to stand against the schemes of the devil. [12] For we do not wrestle against flesh and blood, but against the rulers, against the authorities, against the cosmic powers over this present darkness, against the spiritual forces of evil in the heavenly places. [13] Therefore take up the whole armor of God, that you may be able to withstand in the evil day, and having done all, to stand firm."[6], and that in itself has been taken literally with dire consequences.

Lawyers, Judges, activists, advocates, vigilantes, despots and terrorists have bastardized the Constitution of the United States of America to the point where just like the Bible; they have diluted its efficacy.

The Constitution begins with, "We the people…"; that is the genesis of the most imprecise and ambiguous phrase to possibly ever grace the page of a legal document. Who exactly are *these people*? Were the framers talking about everyone that inhabits these shores, to include Native-Americans, people held in bondage and those people yet to be conquered and left dispossessed from their own land? Did it mean white, European

---

[6] The Holy Bible, English Standard Version Copyright © 2001 by Crossway Bibles, a division of Good News Publishers.

males only or were women to be included? It's definite lack of specificity was in no way an accident. There are some who would argue that the authors deliberately left this description vague to leave room for the evolution of the country and the education and enlightenment of future generations. Or perhaps you can take a more cynical approach and say that it was left intentionally vague to be able to contract the liberties of future non-white male citizens if the opportunity for the exercise of that power becomes available. I am only guessing, but experience has left me to be more agreeable to the latter more so than to the former theory. I don't think altruism was what this homogenous group of individuals had in mind. (They could have had a woman somewhere noted for window dressing, if nothing else!)

"In order to form a more perfect Union…". Please be as kind as to identify the imperfections noted thus far! "Establish Justice, insure domestic Tranquility,….". This implies that before these guys arrived there was no justice or tranquility; or did they import chaos with them?

The plot thickens! "Provide for the common defence,"…; against whom specifically are we preparing the common defense; against the tyranny of England, the bloody Indians (euphemistically described as savages) or were these guys prescient enough to predict a future alien invasion? "Promote the general Welfare, and secure the Blessings of Liberty to ourselves and our Posterity,". What does the concept of the general welfare look like to wealthy landowners who possess acres and acres of land stolen from Native-Americans totally without their *general welfare* in mind? Secure these "Blessings of Liberty", there were a whole lot of people who were not included in the blessing and as the Bible says, if you're not a part of the blessing that means you must be a part of the curse.

Article I

Section. 2

The Constitution, Article I, Section 2. Is the beginning of the ambiguity and with very little research it is easy to ascertain that there is no logical explanation for this section. This business about the use of double negatives is as much bullshit as the people who try to explain it. Throughout the Constitution there are broad and narrow passages of very direct and succinct language, yet apologists try desperately to explain away this glaring anomaly. I'm going to play the conspiracy theorist briefly here, but I neither offer this as fact or probable fiction; just a case for thought. Perhaps the writers decided that in order to keep everyone honest and precluding a person from advancing his own fortune unfairly, let's declare that only a person who is a non-resident can be elected eliminating the temptation to getting elected to serve personal gain.

Section. 3. (Paragraph 3)

"No Person shall be a Senator who shall not have attained to the Age of thirty Years, and been nine Years a Citizen of the United States, and who shall not, when elected, be an Inhabitant of that State for which he shall be chosen."[7]

In this paragraph the confusion is paramount! Scholars have argued that the creators make use of double negatives to effectuate a positive. So in essence they were saying to "who shall not, when elected, be an inhabitant of the State for which he is chosen," and countering that clear and precise legislation with in the preceding portion say,

"No Person…" (first negative), but re-emphasizing "shall not" creating a deliberate entanglement of specificity. If you do some research there are scholars who vehemently argue that this was a style of emphasis common among learned persons well versed in English writing and articulation. I would argue that the evidence does not support that hypothesis evidenced by the extreme level of specificity throughout the rest of the document. Call it what you will but it adds to the confusion.

---

[7] **U.S. National Archives & Records Administration, United States Constitution, Section 3, (Paragraph 3)**
8601 Adelphi Road, College Park, MD, 20740-6001, • 1-86-NARA-NARA • 1-866-272-6272

Section. 8. (Paragraph 4)

"To establish an uniform Rule of Naturalization, and uniform Laws on the subject of Bankruptcies throughout the United States;"[8]

The establishment of a "uniform" Rule of Naturalization has yet to be accomplished, but by beginning the rule of law with the word "To," could suggest that the founders knew that this would be a continual work in progress and being more specific and making definitive pronouncement would limit the powers of government to make adjustments when and as necessary without a successive series of amendments. Very clever and I would argue as a sign of genius! And even though the naturalization process appears uniform as a federal mandate with procedures and regulations, possibly no other portion of the Constitution has been more bastardized with exceptions and exemptions based on biases, privilege and discrimination. Under the guise of immigration restriction throughout the history of this great Republic, the naturalization process has evolved into a procedure designed to be onerous and restrictive. The people who came through Ellis Island would be unable to immigrate to America if the rules were applied uniformly.

Section. 9. (Paragraph 1)

"The Migration or Importation of such Persons as any of the States now existing shall think proper to admit, shall not be prohibited by the Congress prior to the Year one thousand eight hundred and eight, but a Tax or duty may be imposed on such Importation, not exceeding ten dollars for each Person."[9]

Wow! To each make his/her own interpretation! If it walks like a duck, quacks like a duck….. If this is not the precursor to sanction slavery or the forced conscription of persons from location to location as needed, then please "(ex)splain it to me Lucy!"[10]

---

[8] U.S. National Archives & Records Administration, United States Constitution, Section 8, (Paragraph 4)
8601 Adelphi Road, College Park, MD, 20740-6001, • 1-86-NARA-NARA • 1-866-272-6272

[9] U.S. National Archives & Records Administration, United States Constitution, Section 9, (Paragraph 1)
8601 Adelphi Road, College Park, MD, 20740-6001, • 1-86-NARA-NARA • 1-866-272-6272

[10] Paraphrase of an expression by Ricky Ricardo, (Desi Arnez) I Love Lucy (TV Series 1951–1957)

(Paragraph 3)

"No Bill of Attainder or ex post facto Law shall be passed."[11]

A Bill of Attainder is a rule of law stating that the legislature cannot pass a law finding a person guilty of treason or felony without trial. By person did they mean only U.S. citizens? I cite Guantanamo detainees or the alleged participation by the CIA in the execution of Patrice Lumumba, the Prime Minister of the Republic of the Congo after he successfully liberated his country from Belgium or the assassination of an American citizen declared to be a terrorist by the Obama administration while hiding out in Yemen. I am not assigning agreement or outrage to the events cited, just asking; political, Constitutional definitely confusing. To add emphasis to their meaning so as to not in any way be ambiguous the founders include the wording "or ex post facto Law," meaning to disallow retroactive retaliation. Don't get your shorts in a bunch be ye Democrat or Republican; probably every administration since the constitution had been ratified has violated this mandate. Teachers invite your Civics classes to research incidents. I guarantee it will keep them busy for an entire school year.

Article II.

Section. 1. (Paragraph 3, line 1)

"The electors shall meet in their respective States, and vote by Ballots and vote by ballot for two Persons, of whom one at least shall not be an inhabitant of the same State."[12]

Here goes that pesky ambiguous wording again! One shall not be an inhabitant of the state where he/she resides. The 17th Amendment clarifies the procedures for the election of Senators.

AMENDMENT XVII

Passed by Congress May 13, 1912. Ratified April 8, 1913.

Note: Article I, section 3, of the Constitution was modified by the 17th amendment.

"The Senate of the United States shall be composed of two Senators from each State,

---

[11] **U.S. National Archives & Records Administration, United States Constitution, Section 9, (Paragraph 3)**
8601 Adelphi Road, College Park, MD, 20740-6001, • 1-86-NARA-NARA • 1-866-272-6272
[12] **U.S. National Archives & Records Administration, United States Constitution, Article II, Section 1, (Paragraph 1, line 1)**
8601 Adelphi Road, College Park, MD, 20740-6001, • 1-86-NARA-NARA • 1-866-272-6272

elected by the people thereof, for six years; and each Senator shall have one vote. The electors in each State shall have the qualifications requisite for electors of the most numerous branch of the State legislatures.

When vacancies happen in the representation of any State in the Senate, the executive authority of such State shall issue writs of election to fill such vacancies: *Provided*, That the legislature of any State may empower the executive thereof to make temporary appointments until the people fill the vacancies by election as the legislature may direct.

This amendment shall not be so construed as to affect the election or term of any Senator chosen before it becomes valid as part of the Constitution."[13]

Based on this evidence one could surmise that the founders' original intent was superseded by an august legislature and ratified by populations of well-educated citizens, who resided in progressive states.

Ratification by the states (17th Amendment)

Adopted by Congress, the amendment was sent to the states for ratification and was ratified by:

- Massachusetts — May 22, 1912
- Arizona — June 3, 1912
- Minnesota — June 10, 1912
- New York — January 15, 1913
- Kansas — January 17, 1913
- Oregon — January 23, 1913
- North Carolina — January 25, 1913
- California — January 28, 1913
- Michigan — January 28, 1913
- Iowa — January 30, 1913
- Montana — January 30, 1913
- Idaho — January 31, 1913

[13] U.S. National Archives & Records Administration, Amendments to the United States Constitution 11-27, Amendment XVII
8601 Adelphi Road, College Park, MD, 20740-6001, • 1-86-NARA-NARA • 1-866-272-6272
Page URL: http://www.archives.gov/exhibits/charters/constitution_amendments_11-27.html

- West Virginia — February 4, 1913
- Colorado — February 5, 1913
- Nevada — February 6, 1913
- Texas — February 7, 1913
- Washington — February 7, 1913
- Wyoming — February 8, 1913
- Arkansas — February 11, 1913
- Maine — February 11, 1913
- Illinois — February 13, 1913
- North Dakota — February 14, 1913
- Wisconsin — February 18, 1913
- Indiana — February 19, 1913
- New Hampshire — February 19, 1913
- Vermont — February 19, 1913
- South Dakota — February 19, 1913
- Oklahoma — February 24, 1913
- Ohio — February 25, 1913
- Missouri — March 7, 1913
- New Mexico — March 13, 1913
- Nebraska — March 14, 1913
- New Jersey — March 17, 1913
- Tennessee — April 1, 1913
- Pennsylvania — April 2, 1913
- Connecticut — April 8, 1913

The amendment was rejected by:

- Utah — February 26, 1913

- Delaware — March 18, 1913

Thirty-six states ratified the Seventeenth Amendment, certification by Secretary of State William Jennings Bryan on May 31, 1913, as part of the Constitution.

The amendment has subsequently been ratified by:

- Louisiana — June 11, 1914

- Alabama — April 11, 2002

- Delaware — July 1, 2010

- Maryland — April 1, 2012

No action on the amendment has been completed by:

- Florida

- Georgia

- Kentucky

- Mississippi

- Rhode Island

- South Carolina

- Virginia[14]

  * This mystery would be solved except for the fact that the 17th Amendment was conceived for entirely different reasons than the correction of the original wording about where the electors inhabit.

Article III.

---

[14] James J. Kilpatrick, ed. (1961). *The Constitution of the United States and Amendments Thereto*. Virginia Commission on Constitutional Government. p. 49.

Section. 1.

"The judicial Power of the United States shall be vested in one supreme Court, and in such inferior Courts as the Congress may from time to time ordain and establish. The Judges, both of the supreme and inferior Courts, shall hold their Offices during good Behaviour,....."[15]

This section addresses judicial power and 'inferior courts.' What pray tell is "good Behaviour," and the omission of what constitutes 'bad' behavior opens the door to individual interpretation, which is why we euphemistically say Justices are appointed for life.

Would the conduct of Justices and their demeanor include the bizarre behavior of Justices Clarence Thomas and Antonin Scalia or would the lack of bona fides from a widely accepted Ivy League school by Justice Thurgood Marshall be considered bad? The loose wording makes the interpretation a matter of perception and the practice of politics feeds the confusion.

*There are other parts of the Articles and Sections equally subject to interpretation that may or may not have been deliberately vague or so nonspecific as to give Constitutional scholars many years for debate and application to vex the most righteous and humanely moral persons. The best test of one's own political acuity is how well one perceives the intent versus the reality of application.

---

[15] U.S. National Archives & Records Administration, United States Constitution, Article III, Section 1, Paragraph 1
8601 Adelphi Road, College Park, MD, 20740-6001, • 1-86-NARA-NARA • 1-866-272-6272

THE U.S. NATIONAL ARCHIVES & RECORDS ADMINISTRATION

www.archives.gov

The Bill of Rights: A Transcription

The Preamble to The Bill of Rights

Congress of the United States
begun and held at the City of New-York, on
Wednesday the fourth of March, one thousand seven hundred and eighty nine.

THE Conventions of a number of the States, having at the time of their adopting the Constitution, expressed a desire, in order to prevent misconstruction or abuse of its powers, that further declaratory and restrictive clauses should be added: And as extending the ground of public confidence in the Government, will best ensure the beneficent ends of its institution.

RESOLVED by the Senate and House of Representatives of the United States of America, in Congress assembled, two thirds of both Houses concurring, that the following Articles be proposed to the Legislatures of the several States, as amendments to the Constitution of the United States, all, or any of which Articles, when ratified by three fourths of the said Legislatures, to be valid to all intents and purposes, as part of the said Constitution; viz.

ARTICLES in addition to, and Amendment of the Constitution of the United States of America, proposed by Congress, and ratified by the Legislatures of the several States, pursuant to the fifth Article of the original Constitution.

Note: The following text is a transcription of the first ten amendments to the Constitution in their original form. These amendments were ratified December 15, 1791, and form what is known as the "Bill of Rights."

Amendment I

Congress shall make no law respecting an establishment of religion, or prohibiting the free exercise thereof; or abridging the freedom of speech, or of the press; or the right of the people peaceably to assemble, and to petition the Government for a redress of grievances.

Amendment II

A well regulated Militia, being necessary to the security of a free State, the right of the people to keep and bear Arms, shall not be infringed.

Amendment III

No Soldier shall, in time of peace be quartered in any house, without the consent of the Owner, nor in time of war, but in a manner to be prescribed by law.

Amendment IV

The right of the people to be secure in their persons, houses, papers, and effects, against unreasonable searches and seizures, shall not be violated, and no Warrants shall issue, but upon probable cause, supported by Oath or affirmation, and particularly describing the place to be searched, and the persons or things to be seized.

Amendment V

No person shall be held to answer for a capital, or otherwise infamous crime, unless on a presentment or indictment of a Grand Jury, except in cases arising in the land or naval forces, or in the Militia, when in actual service in time of War or public danger; nor shall any person be subject for the same offence to be twice put in jeopardy of life or limb; nor shall be compelled in any criminal case to be a witness against himself, nor be deprived of life, liberty, or property, without due process of law; nor shall private property be taken for public use, without just compensation.

Amendment VI

In all criminal prosecutions, the accused shall enjoy the right to a speedy and public trial, by an impartial jury of the State and district wherein the crime shall have been committed, which district shall have been previously ascertained by law, and to be informed of the nature and cause of the accusation; to be confronted with the witnesses against him; to have compulsory process for obtaining witnesses in his favor, and to have the Assistance of Counsel for his defence.

Amendment VII

In Suits at common law, where the value in controversy shall exceed twenty dollars, the right of trial by jury shall be preserved, and no fact tried by a jury, shall be otherwise re-examined in any Court of the United States, than according to the rules of the common law.

Amendment VIII

Excessive bail shall not be required, nor excessive fines imposed, nor cruel and unusual punishments inflicted.

Amendment IX

The enumeration in the Constitution, of certain rights, shall not be construed to deny or disparage others retained by the people.

Amendment X

The powers not delegated to the United States by the Constitution, nor prohibited by it to the States, are reserved to the States respectively, or to the people.[16]

---

[16]

Note: The capitalization and punctuation in this version is from the enrolled original of the Joint Resolution of Congress proposing the Bill of Rights, which is on permanent display in the Rotunda of the National Archives Building, Washington, D.C.

Page URL: http://www.archives.gov/exhibits/charters/bill_of_rights_transcript.html

U.S. National Archives & Records Administration
8601 Adelphi Road, College Park, MD, 20740-6001, • 1-86-NARA-NARA • 1-866-272-6272

THE U.S. NATIONAL ARCHIVES & RECORDS ADMINISTRATION

www.archives.govSeptember 9, 2013

The Constitution: Amendments 11-27

Constitutional Amendments 1-10 make up what is known as The Bill of Rights. Amendments 11-27 are listed below.

AMENDMENT XI

Passed by Congress March 4, 1794. Ratified February 7, 1795.

Note: Article III, section 2, of the Constitution was modified by amendment 11.

The Judicial power of the United States shall not be construed to extend to any suit in law or equity, commenced or prosecuted against one of the United States by Citizens of another State, or by Citizens or Subjects of any Foreign State.

AMENDMENT XII

Passed by Congress December 9, 1803. Ratified June 15, 1804.

Note: A portion of Article II, section 1 of the Constitution was superseded by the 12th amendment.

The Electors shall meet in their respective states and vote by ballot for President and Vice-President, one of whom, at least, shall not be an inhabitant of the same state with themselves; they shall name in their ballots the person voted for as President, and in distinct ballots the person voted for as Vice-President, and they shall make distinct lists of all persons voted for as President, and of all persons voted for as Vice-President, and of the number of votes for each, which lists they shall sign and certify, and transmit sealed to the seat of the government of the United States, directed to the President of the Senate; -- the President of the Senate shall, in the presence of the Senate and House of Representatives, open all the certificates and the votes shall then be counted; -- The person having the greatest number of votes for President, shall be the President, if such number be a majority of the whole number of Electors appointed; and if no person have such majority, then from the persons having the highest numbers not exceeding three on the list of those voted for as President, the House of Representatives shall choose immediately, by ballot, the President. But in choosing the President, the votes shall be taken by states, the representation from each state having one vote; a quorum for this purpose shall consist of a member or members from two-thirds of the states, and a majority of all the states shall be necessary to a choice. [And if the House of Representatives shall not choose a President whenever the right of choice shall devolve upon them, before the fourth day of March next following, then the Vice-President shall act as President, as in case of the death or other constitutional disability of the President. --]* The person having the greatest number of votes as Vice-President, shall be the Vice-President, if such number be a majority of the whole number of Electors appointed, and if no person have a majority, then from the two highest numbers on the list, the Senate shall choose the Vice-President; a quorum for the purpose shall consist of two-thirds of the whole number of Senators, and a majority of the whole number shall be necessary to a choice. But no person constitutionally ineligible to the office of President shall be eligible to that of Vice-President of the United States.

Superseded by section 3 of the 20th amendment.

AMENDMENT XIII

Passed by Congress January 31, 1865. Ratified December 6, 1865.

Note: A portion of Article IV, section 2, of the Constitution was superseded by the 13th amendment.

Section 1.
Neither slavery nor involuntary servitude, except as a punishment for crime whereof the party shall have been duly convicted, shall exist within the United States, or any place subject to their jurisdiction.

Section 2.
Congress shall have power to enforce this article by appropriate legislation.

AMENDMENT XIV

Passed by Congress June 13, 1866. Ratified July 9, 1868.

Note: Article I, section 2, of the Constitution was modified by section 2 of the 14th amendment.

Section 1.
All persons born or naturalized in the United States, and subject to the jurisdiction thereof, are citizens of the United States and of the State wherein they reside. No State shall make or enforce any law which shall abridge the privileges or immunities of citizens of the United States; nor shall any State deprive any person of life, liberty, or property, without due process of law; nor deny to any person within its jurisdiction the equal protection of the laws.

Section 2.
Representatives shall be apportioned among the several States according to their respective numbers, counting the whole number of persons in each State, excluding Indians not taxed. But when the right to vote at any election for the choice of electors for President and

Vice-President of the United States, Representatives in Congress, the Executive and Judicial officers of a State, or the members of the Legislature thereof, is denied to any of the male inhabitants of such State, being twenty-one years of age,* and citizens of the United States, or in any way abridged, except for participation in rebellion, or other crime, the basis of representation therein shall be reduced in the proportion which the number of such male citizens shall bear to the whole number of male citizens twenty-one years of age in such State.

Section 3.
No person shall be a Senator or Representative in Congress, or elector of President and Vice-President, or hold any office, civil or military, under the United States, or under any State, who, having previously taken an oath, as a member of Congress, or as an officer of the United States, or as a member of any State legislature, or as an executive or judicial officer of any State, to support the Constitution of the United States, shall have engaged in insurrection or rebellion against the same, or given aid or comfort to the enemies thereof. But Congress may by a vote of two-thirds of each House, remove such disability.

Section 4.
The validity of the public debt of the United States, authorized by law, including debts incurred for payment of pensions and bounties for services in suppressing insurrection or rebellion, shall not be questioned. But neither the United States nor any State shall assume or pay any debt or obligation incurred in aid of insurrection or rebellion against the United States, or any claim for the loss or emancipation of any slave; but all such debts, obligations and claims shall be held illegal and void.

Section 5.
The Congress shall have the power to enforce, by appropriate legislation, the provisions of this article.

*Changed by section 1 of the 26th amendment.

AMENDMENT XV

Passed by Congress February 26, 1869. Ratified February 3, 1870.

Section 1.
The right of citizens of the United States to vote shall not be denied or abridged by the United States or by any State on account of race, color, or previous condition of servitude--

Section 2.
The Congress shall have the power to enforce this article by appropriate legislation.

AMENDMENT XVI

Passed by Congress July 2, 1909. Ratified February 3, 1913.

Note: Article I, section 9, of the Constitution was modified by amendment 16.

The Congress shall have power to lay and collect taxes on incomes, from whatever source derived, without apportionment among the several States, and without regard to any census or enumeration.

AMENDMENT XVII

Passed by Congress May 13, 1912. Ratified April 8, 1913.

Note: Article I, section 3, of the Constitution was modified by the 17th amendment.

The Senate of the United States shall be composed of two Senators from each State, elected by the people thereof, for six years; and each Senator shall have one vote. The electors in each State shall have the qualifications requisite for electors of the most numerous branch of the State legislatures.

When vacancies happen in the representation of any State in the Senate, the executive authority of such State shall issue writs of election to fill such vacancies: *Provided*, That the legislature of any State may empower the executive thereof to make temporary appointments until the people fill the vacancies by election as the legislature may direct.

This amendment shall not be so construed as to affect the election or term of any Senator chosen before it becomes valid as part of the Constitution.

AMENDMENT XVIII

Passed by Congress December 18, 1917. Ratified January 16, 1919. Repealed by amendment 21.

Section 1.
After one year from the ratification of this article the manufacture, sale, or transportation of intoxicating liquors within, the importation thereof into, or the exportation thereof from the United States and all territory subject to the jurisdiction thereof for beverage purposes is hereby prohibited.

Section 2.
The Congress and the several States shall have concurrent power to enforce this article by appropriate legislation.

Section 3.
This article shall be inoperative unless it shall have been ratified as an amendment to the Constitution by the legislatures of the several States, as provided in the Constitution, within seven years from the date of the submission hereof to the States by the Congress.

AMENDMENT XIX

Passed by Congress June 4, 1919. Ratified August 18, 1920.

The right of citizens of the United States to vote shall not be denied or abridged by the United States or by any State on account of sex.

Congress shall have power to enforce this article by appropriate legislation.

AMENDMENT XX

Passed by Congress March 2, 1932. Ratified January 23, 1933.

Note: Article I, section 4, of the Constitution was modified by section 2 of this amendment. In addition, a portion of the 12th amendment was superseded by section 3.

Section 1.
The terms of the President and the Vice President shall end at noon on the 20th day of January, and the terms of Senators and Representatives at noon on the 3rd day of January, of the years in which such terms would have ended if this article had not been ratified; and the terms of their successors shall then begin.

Section 2.
The Congress shall assemble at least once in every year, and such meeting shall begin at noon on the 3d day of January, unless they shall by law appoint a different day.

Section 3.
If, at the time fixed for the beginning of the term of the President, the President elect shall have died, the Vice President elect shall become President. If a President shall not have been chosen before the time fixed for the beginning of his term, or if the President elect shall have failed to qualify, then the Vice President elect shall act as President until a President shall have qualified; and the Congress may by law provide for the case wherein neither a President elect nor a Vice President shall have qualified, declaring who shall then act as President, or the manner in which one who is to act shall be selected, and such person shall act accordingly until a President or Vice President shall have qualified.

Section 4.
The Congress may by law provide for the case of the death of any of the persons from whom the House of Representatives may choose a President whenever the right of choice shall have devolved upon them, and for the case of the death of any of the persons from whom the Senate may choose a Vice President whenever the right of choice shall have devolved upon them.

Section 5.
Sections 1 and 2 shall take effect on the 15th day of October following the ratification of this article.

Section 6.
This article shall be inoperative unless it shall have been ratified as an amendment to the Constitution by the legislatures of three-fourths of the several States within seven years from the date of its submission.

AMENDMENT XXI

Passed by Congress February 20, 1933. Ratified December 5, 1933.

Section 1.
The eighteenth article of amendment to the Constitution of the United States is hereby re-

pealed.

Section 2.
The transportation or importation into any State, Territory, or Possession of the United States for delivery or use therein of intoxicating liquors, in violation of the laws thereof, is hereby prohibited.

Section 3.
This article shall be inoperative unless it shall have been ratified as an amendment to the Constitution by conventions in the several States, as provided in the Constitution, within seven years from the date of the submission hereof to the States by the Congress.

AMENDMENT XXII

Passed by Congress March 21, 1947. Ratified February 27, 1951.

Section 1.
No person shall be elected to the office of the President more than twice, and no person who has held the office of President, or acted as President, for more than two years of a term to which some other person was elected President shall be elected to the office of President more than once. But this Article shall not apply to any person holding the office of President when this Article was proposed by Congress, and shall not prevent any person who may be holding the office of President, or acting as President, during the term within which this Article becomes operative from holding the office of President or acting as President during the remainder of such term.

Section 2.
This article shall be inoperative unless it shall have been ratified as an amendment to the Constitution by the legislatures of three-fourths of the several States within seven years from the date of its submission to the States by the Congress.

AMENDMENT XXIII

Passed by Congress June 16, 1960. Ratified March 29, 1961.

Section 1.
The District constituting the seat of Government of the United States shall appoint in such manner as Congress may direct:

A number of electors of President and Vice President equal to the whole number of Senators and Representatives in Congress to which the District would be entitled if it were a State, but in no event more than the least populous State; they shall be in addition to those appointed by the States, but they shall be considered, for the purposes of the election of President and Vice President, to be electors appointed by a State; and they shall meet in the District and perform such duties as provided by the twelfth article of amendment.

Section 2.
The Congress shall have power to enforce this article by appropriate legislation.

AMENDMENT XXIV

Passed by Congress August 27, 1962. Ratified January 23, 1964.

Section 1.
The right of citizens of the United States to vote in any primary or other election for President or Vice President, for electors for President or Vice President, or for Senator or Representative in Congress, shall not be denied or abridged by the United States or any State by reason of failure to pay poll tax or other tax.

Section 2.
The Congress shall have power to enforce this article by appropriate legislation.

AMENDMENT XXV

Passed by Congress July 6, 1965. Ratified February 10, 1967.

Note: Article II, section 1, of the Constitution was affected by the 25th amendment.

Section 1.
In case of the removal of the President from office or of his death or resignation, the Vice President shall become President.

Section 2.
Whenever there is a vacancy in the office of the Vice President, the President shall nominate a Vice President who shall take office upon confirmation by a majority vote of both Houses of Congress.

Section 3.
Whenever the President transmits to the President pro tempore of the Senate and the Speaker of the House of Representatives his written declaration that he is unable to discharge the powers and duties of his office, and until he transmits to them a written declaration to the contrary, such powers and duties shall be discharged by the Vice President as Acting President.

Section 4.
Whenever the Vice President and a majority of either the principal officers of the executive departments or of such other body as Congress may by law provide, transmit to the President pro tempore of the Senate and the Speaker of the House of Representatives their written declaration that the President is unable to discharge the powers and duties of his office, the Vice President shall immediately assume the powers and duties of the office as Acting President.

Thereafter, when the President transmits to the President pro tempore of the Senate and the Speaker of the House of Representatives his written declaration that no inability exists, he shall resume the powers and duties of his office unless the Vice President and a majority of either the principal officers of the executive department or of such other body as Congress may by law provide, transmit within four days to the President pro tempore of the Senate and the Speaker of the House of Representatives their written declaration that the President is unable to discharge the powers and duties of his office. Thereupon Congress shall decide the issue, assembling within forty-eight hours for that purpose if not in session. If the Congress, within twenty-one days after receipt of the latter written declaration, or, if Congress is not in session, within twenty-one days after Congress is required to assemble, determines by two-thirds vote of both Houses that the President is unable to discharge the powers and duties of his office, the Vice President shall continue to discharge the same as Acting President; otherwise, the President shall resume the powers and duties of his office.

AMENDMENT XXVI

Passed by Congress March 23, 1971. Ratified July 1, 1971.

Note: Amendment 14, section 2, of the Constitution was modified by section 1 of the 26th amendment.

Section 1.
The right of citizens of the United States, who are eighteen years of age or older, to vote shall not be denied or abridged by the United States or by any State on account of age.

Section 2.
The Congress shall have power to enforce this article by appropriate legislation.

AMENDMENT XXVII

Originally proposed Sept. 25, 1789. Ratified May 7, 1992.

No law, varying the compensation for the services of the Senators and Representatives, shall take effect, until an election of representatives shall have intervened. [17]

A brief look at each amendment reveals that the original intent was insufficient and needed some alterations to fit the changing fabric of the new nation.

---

[17] AMENDMENT XXVII *Ratified May 7, 1992.*

Page URL: http://www.archives.gov/exhibits/charters/constitution_amendments_11-27.html

---

U.S. National Archives & Records Administration
8601 Adelphi Road, College Park, MD, 20740-6001, • 1-86-NARA-NARA • 1-866-272-6272

The fact that a mechanism was available to make amendments woven into the original document suggests that even though some people believed that these guys walked on water, they themselves were not as arrogant and narcissistic as we would like to believe. I would be first to admit that the originators were genii from a legal perspective in planning for the eventual future litigation that was surely to come. American jurisprudence is foundationally tied to this document in both intent and formulation.

First the Preamble:

"**THE** Conventions of a number of the States, having at the time of their adopting the Constitution, expressed a desire, in order to prevent misconstruction or abuse of its powers, that further declaratory and restrictive clauses should be added: And as extending the ground of public confidence in the Government, will best ensure the beneficent ends of its institution."[18]

Within 8 words into the preamble, ambiguity was both deliberate and cleverly inserted into the text. The numbers of states was left imprecise; in spite an exact number was available for reporting. "(E) expressed a desire…."; really a desire? I doubt for a minute that the originators acquiesced to desires except in their sex lives or their thirst for good bourbon.

Prevent misconstruction; the document was already constructed, so how do you prevent misconstruction? The next part should have been made stronger, "or abuse of its powers…," which should have read "or punishable by death!" These four words may have prevented billions of dollars in money and man hours over frivolous arguments based on Constitutional interpretation. The last sentence is unique and about as solid as wording can get, even suggesting moral elevation uncommon for men whose values were pre-ordained by status.

---

[18] **U.S. National Archives & Records Administration**
8601 Adelphi Road, College Park, MD, 20740-6001, • 1-86-NARA-NARA • 1-866-272-6272

Amendment I: The first and perhaps most mis-interpreted when quoted by individuals or organizations who seek to use it for the basis of the rights of free speech exclusively. "Make no laws respecting establishment of religion,"

Here is an article taken from the Washington Post:

What part of 'no law respecting an establishment of religion' does North Carolina not understand?

By Barry W. Lynn, April 04, 2013

The North Carolina legislature return to work Wednesday, Jan. 30, 2013. (Takaaki Iwabu/AP)

Imagine driving from Northern Virginia to the Outer Banks in North Carolina, and as you hit the state line, you see a large highway sign that reads: "Welcome To North Carolina: A Christian State," complete with an iconic image of Jesus on a cross.

This incredible scenario could become a reality if misguided lawmakers in Raleigh succeed in passing a bill that says the state and all of its subsidiary groups (including public schools) are free to make any laws they choose regarding religion. That's right; they could even declare an official faith.

House Joint Resolution 494, known was the "Rowan County Defense of Religion Act," makes the claim that "each state is sovereign and may independently determine how the state may make laws respecting an establishment of religion."[19]

Prayer in the Public Schools

The issue: What limitations does the Establishment Clause place on prayer in public schools?

"The question of school-sponsored prayer has proven highly controversial. In the landmark case of *Engel v Vitale* in 1962, the Court ruled that New York's practice of beginning school days with a prayer drafted by school officials violated the Establishment Clause. This is the case, the Court said, whether or not students are given the option of not participating in the prayer. Writing for the Court, Justice Black said the Establishment Clause was violated when school put "indirect coercive pressure upon religious minorities to conform to the officially approved religion." Peer pressure being as strong as it is among the young, many students who might otherwise choose not to participate in prayer will do so for fear of otherwise being seeing as an oddball."[20]

Cases

Engel v Vitale (1962)
Wallace v Jaffree (1985)
Lee v Weisman (1992)
Santa Fe Indep. School Dist. v Doe (2000)

---

[19] Washington Post, By Barry W. Lynn, April 04, 2013, What part of 'no law respecting an establishment of religion' does North Carolina not understand?

[20] http://law2.umkc.edu/faculty/projects/ftrials/conlaw/schoolprayer.html

Analyzing the Vision of the Founding Fathers

"By three methods we may learn wisdom: First, by reflection, which is noblest; Second, by imitation, which is easiest; and third by experience, which is the bitterest."

Confucius

THE U.S. NATIONAL ARCHIVES & RECORDS ADMINISTRATION

www.archives.gov

The Declaration of Independence: A Transcription

IN CONGRESS, July 4, 1776.

The unanimous Declaration of the thirteen united States of America,

When in the Course of human events, it becomes necessary for one people to dissolve the political bands which have connected them with another, and to assume among the powers of the earth, the separate and equal station to which the Laws of Nature and of Nature's God entitle them, a decent respect to the opinions of mankind requires that they should declare the causes which impel them to the separation.

We hold these truths to be self-evident, that all men are created equal, that they are endowed by their Creator with certain unalienable Rights, that among these are Life, Liberty and the pursuit of Happiness.--That to secure these rights, Governments are instituted among Men, deriving their just powers from the consent of the governed, --That whenever any Form of Government becomes destructive of these ends, it is the Right of the People to alter or to abolish it, and to institute new Government, laying its foundation on such principles and organizing its powers in such form, as to them shall seem most likely to effect their Safety and Happiness. Prudence, indeed, will dictate that Governments long established should not be changed for light and transient causes; and accordingly all experience hath shewn, that mankind are more disposed to suffer, while evils are sufferable, than to right themselves by abolishing the forms to which they are accustomed. But when a long train of abuses and usurpations, pursuing invariably the same Object evinces a design to reduce them under absolute Despotism, it is their right, it is their duty, to throw off such Government, and to provide new Guards for their future security.--Such has been the patient sufferance of these Colonies; and such is now the necessity which constrains them to alter their former Systems of Government. The history of the present King of Great Britain is a history of repeated injuries and usurpations, all having in direct object the establishment of an absolute Tyranny over these States. To prove this, let Facts be submitted to a candid world.

He has refused his Assent to Laws, the most wholesome and necessary for the public good.

He has forbidden his Governors to pass Laws of immediate and pressing importance, unless suspended in their operation till his Assent should be obtained; and when so suspended, he has utterly neglected to attend to them.

He has refused to pass other Laws for the accommodation of large districts of people, unless those people would relinquish the right of Representation in the Legislature, a right inestimable to them and formidable to tyrants only.

He has called together legislative bodies at places unusual, uncomfortable, and distant from the depository of their public Records, for the sole purpose of fatiguing them into compliance with his measures.

He has dissolved Representative Houses repeatedly, for opposing with manly firmness his invasions on the rights of the people.

He has refused for a long time, after such dissolutions, to cause others to be elected; whereby the Legislative powers, incapable of Annihilation, have returned to the People at large for their exercise; the State remaining in the mean time exposed to all the dangers of invasion from without, and convulsions within.

He has endeavoured to prevent the population of these States; for that purpose obstructing the Laws for Naturalization of Foreigners; refusing to pass others to encourage their migrations hither, and raising the conditions of new Appropriations of Lands.

He has obstructed the Administration of Justice, by refusing his Assent to Laws for establishing Judiciary powers.

He has made Judges dependent on his Will alone, for the tenure of their offices, and the amount and payment of their salaries.

He has erected a multitude of New Offices, and sent hither swarms of Officers to harrass our people, and eat out their substance.

He has kept among us, in times of peace, Standing Armies without the Consent of our legislatures.

He has affected to render the Military independent of and superior to the Civil power.

He has combined with others to subject us to a jurisdiction foreign to our constitution, and unacknowledged by our laws; giving his Assent to their Acts of pretended Legislation:
For Quartering large bodies of armed troops among us:
For protecting them, by a mock Trial, from punishment for any Murders which they should commit on the Inhabitants of these States:
For cutting off our Trade with all parts of the world:
For imposing Taxes on us without our Consent:
For depriving us in many cases, of the benefits of Trial by Jury:
For transporting us beyond Seas to be tried for pretended offences
For abolishing the free System of English Laws in a neighbouring Province, establishing therein an Arbitrary government, and enlarging its Boundaries so as to render it at once an example and fit instrument for introducing the same absolute rule into these Colonies:
For taking away our Charters, abolishing our most valuable Laws, and altering fundamentally the Forms of our Governments:
For suspending our own Legislatures, and declaring themselves invested with power to legislate for us in all cases whatsoever.
He has abdicated Government here, by declaring us out of his Protection and waging War against us.
He has plundered our seas, ravaged our Coasts, burnt our towns, and destroyed the lives of our people.
He is at this time transporting large Armies of foreign Mercenaries to compleat the works of death, desolation and tyranny, already begun with circumstances of Cruelty & perfidy scarcely paralleled in the most barbarous ages, and totally unworthy the Head of a civilized nation.
He has constrained our fellow Citizens taken Captive on the high Seas to bear Arms against their Country, to become the executioners of their friends and Brethren, or to fall themselves by their Hands.
He has excited domestic insurrections amongst us, and has endeavoured to bring on the inhabitants of our frontiers, the merciless Indian Savages, whose known rule of warfare, is an undistinguished destruction of all ages, sexes and conditions.

In every stage of these Oppressions We have Petitioned for Redress in the most humble terms: Our repeated Petitions have been answered only by repeated injury. A Prince whose character is thus marked by every act which may define a Tyrant, is unfit to be the ruler of a free people.

Nor have We been wanting in attentions to our Brittish brethren. We have warned them from time to time of attempts by their legislature to extend an unwarrantable jurisdiction over us. We have reminded them of the circumstances of our emigration and settlement here. We have appealed to their native justice and magnanimity, and we have conjured them by the ties of our common kindred to disavow these usurpations, which, would inevitably interrupt our connections and correspondence. They too have been deaf to the voice of justice and of consanguinity. We must, therefore, acquiesce in the necessity, which denounces our Separation, and hold them, as we hold the rest of mankind, Enemies in War, in Peace Friends.

We, therefore, the Representatives of the united States of America, in General Congress, Assembled, appealing to the Supreme Judge of the world for the rectitude of our intentions, do, in the Name, and by Authority of the good People of these Colonies, solemnly publish and declare, That these United Colonies are, and of Right ought to be Free and Independent States; that they are Absolved from all Allegiance to the British Crown, and that all political connection between them and the State of Great Britain, is and ought to be totally dissolved; and that as Free and Independent States, they have full Power to levy War, conclude Peace, contract Alliances, establish Commerce, and to do all other Acts and Things which Independent States may of right do. And for the support of this Declaration, with a firm reliance on the protection of divine Providence, we mutually pledge to each other our Lives, our Fortunes and our sacred Honor.

The 56 signatures on the Declaration appear in the positions indicated:

Column 1
Georgia:
  Button Gwinnett
  Lyman Hall
  George Walton

Column 2
North Carolina:
  William Hooper
  Joseph Hewes
  John Penn
South Carolina:
  Edward Rutledge
  Thomas Heyward, Jr.
  Thomas Lynch, Jr.
  Arthur Middleton

Column 3
Massachusetts:
John Hancock
Maryland:
Samuel Chase
William Paca
Thomas Stone
Charles Carroll of Carrollton
Virginia:
George Wythe
Richard Henry Lee
Thomas Jefferson
Benjamin Harrison
Thomas Nelson, Jr.
Francis Lightfoot Lee
Carter Braxton

Column 4
Pennsylvania:
  Robert Morris
  Benjamin Rush
  Benjamin Franklin
  John Morton
  George Clymer
  James Smith
  George Taylor
  James Wilson
  George Ross
Delaware:
  Caesar Rodney

George Read
Thomas McKean

Column 5
New York:
William Floyd
Philip Livingston
Francis Lewis
Lewis Morris
New Jersey:
Richard Stockton
John Witherspoon
Francis Hopkinson
John Hart
Abraham Clark

Column 6
New Hampshire:
Josiah Bartlett
William Whipple
Massachusetts:
Samuel Adams
John Adams
Robert Treat Paine
Elbridge Gerry
Rhode Island:
Stephen Hopkins
William Ellery
Connecticut:
Roger Sherman
Samuel Huntington
William Williams
Oliver Wolcott
New Hampshire:
Matthew Thornton[21]

21

Page URL: http://www.archives.gov/exhibits/charters/declaration_transcript.html

U.S. National Archives & Records Administration
8601 Adelphi Road, College Park, MD, 20740-6001, • 1-86-NARA-NARA • 1-866-272-6272

Historical Dissemination of Information
(Famous Documents Gone Unrecognized or Deliberately Ignored)

"No matter how busy you may think you are, you must find time for reading, or surrender yourself to self-chosen ignorance."

Confucius

1869) Frederick Douglass Describes The "Composite Nation"

Image Ownership: Public Domain

In an 1869 speech in Boston, Frederick Douglass challenged most social observers and politicians (including most African Americans) by advocating the acceptance of Chinese immigration. His argument is presented below.

As nations are among the largest and the most complete divisions into which society is formed, the grandest aggregations of organized human power; as they raise to observation and distinction the world's greatest men, and call into requisition the highest order of talent and ability for their guidance, preservation and success, they are ever among the most attractive, instructive and useful subjects of thought, to those just entering upon the duties and activities of life.

The simple organization of a people into a National body, composite or otherwise, is of itself and impressive fact. As an original proceeding, it marks the point of departure of a people, from the darkness and chaos of unbridled barbarism, to the wholesome restraints of public law and society. It implies a willing surrender and subjection of individual aims and ends, often narrow and selfish, to the broader and better ones that arise out of society as a whole. It is both a sign and a result of civilization.

A knowledge of the character, resources and proceedings of other nations, affords us the means of comparison and criticism, without which progress would be feeble, tardy, and perhaps, impossible. It is by comparing one nation with another, and one learning from another, each competing with all, and all competing with each, that hurtful errors are exposed, great social truths discovered, and the wheels of civilization whirled onward.

I am especially to speak to you of the character and mission of the United States, with special reference to the question whether we are the better or the worse for being composed of different races of men. I propose to consider first, what we are, second, what we are likely to be, and, thirdly, what we ought to be.

Without undue vanity or unjust depreciation of others, we may claim to be, in many respects, the most fortunate of nations. We stand in relation to all others, as youth to age. Other nations have had their day of greatness and glory; we are yet to have our day, and that day is coming. The dawn is already upon us. It is bright and full of promise. Other nations have reached their culminating point. We are at the beginning of our ascent. They have apparently exhausted the conditions essential to their further growth and extension, while we are abundant in all the material essential to further national growth and greatness.

The resources of European statesmanship are now sorely taxed to maintain their nationalities at their ancient height of greatness and power.

American statesmanship, worthy of the name, is now taxing its energies to frame measures to meet the demands of constantly increasing expansion of power, responsibility and duty.

Without fault or merit on either side, theirs or ours, the balance is largely in our favor. Like the grand old forests, renewed and enriched from decaying trunks once full of life and beauty, but now moss-covered, oozy and crumbling, we are destined to grow and flourish while they decline and fade.

This is one view of American position and destiny. It is proper to notice that it is not the only view. Different opinions and conflicting judgments meet us here, as elsewhere.

It is thought by many, and said by some, that this Republic has already seen its best days; that the historian may now write the story of its decline and fall.

Two classes of men are just now especially afflicted with such forebodings. The first are those who are croakers by nature—the men who have a taste for funerals, and especially National funerals. They never see the bright side of anything and probably never will. Like the raven in the lines of Edgar A. Poe they have learned two words, and these are "never more." They usually begin by telling us what we never shall see. Their little speeches are about as follows: You will never see such Statesmen in the councils of the nation as Clay, Calhoun and Webster. You will never see the South morally reconstructed and our once happy people again united. You will never see the Government harmonious and successful while in the hands of different races. You will never make the negro work without a master, or make him an intelligent voter, or a good and useful citizen. The last never is generally the parent of all the other little nevers that follow.

During the late contest for the Union, the air was full of nevers, every one of which was contradicted and put to shame by the result, and I doubt not that most of those we now hear in our troubled air, will meet the same fate.

It is probably well for us that some of our gloomy prophets are limited in their powers, to prediction. Could they command the destructive bolt, as readily as they command the destructive world, it is hard to say what might happen to the country. They might fulfill their own gloomy prophesies. Of course it is easy to see why certain other classes on men speak hopelessly concerning us.

A Government founded upon justice, and recognizing the equal rights of all men; claiming higher authority for existence, or sanction for its laws, that nature, reason, and the regularly ascertained will of the people; steadily refusing to put its sword and purse in the service of any religious creed or family is a standing offense to most of the Governments of the world, and to some narrow and bigoted people among ourselves.

To those who doubt and deny the preponderance of good over evil in human nature; who think the few are made to rule, and many to serve; who put rank above brotherhood, and race above humanity; who attach more importance to ancient forms than to the living realities of the present; who worship power in whatever hands it may be lodged and by whatever means it may have been obtained; our Government is a mountain of sin, and, what is worse, its [sic] seems confirmed in its transgressions.

One of the latest and most potent European prophets, one who has felt himself called upon for a special deliverance concerning us and our destiny as a nation, was the late Thomas Carlyle. He described us as rushing to ruin, not only with determined purpose, but with desperate velocity.

How long we have been on this high road to ruin, and when we may expect to reach the terrible end our gloomy prophet, enveloped in the fogs of London, has not been pleased to tell us.

Warnings and advice are not to be despised, from any quarter, and especially not from one so eminent as Mr. Carlyle; and yet Americans will find it hard to heed even men like him, if there be any in the world like him, while the animus is so apparent, bitter and perverse.

A man to whom despotism is Savior and Liberty the destroyer of society,—who, during the last twenty years of his life, in every contest between liberty and oppression, uniformly and promptly took sides with the oppressor; who regarded every extension of the right of suffrage, even to white men in his own country, as shooting Niagara; who gloats over deeds of cruelty, and talked of applying to the backs of men the beneficent whip, to the great delight of many, the slave drivers of America in particular, could have little sympathy with our Emancipated and progressive Republic, or with the triumphs of liberty anywhere.

But the American people can easily stand the utterances of such a man. They however have a right to be impatient and indignant at those among ourselves who turn the most hopeful portents into omens of disaster, and make themselves the ministers of despair when they should be those of hope, and help cheer on the country in the new and grand career of justice upon which it has now so nobly and bravely entered. Of errors and defects we certainly have not less than our full share, enough to keep the reformer awake, the statesman busy, and the country in a pretty lively state of agitation for some time to come. Perfection is an object to be aimed at by all, but it is not an attribute of any form of Government. Neutrality is the law for all. Something different, something better, or something worse may come, but so far as respects our present system and form of Government, and the altitude we occupy, we need not shrink from comparison with any nation of our times. We are today the best fed, the best clothed, the best sheltered and the best instructed people in the world.

There was a time when even brave men might look fearfully at the destiny of the Republic. When our country was involved in a tangled network of contradictions; when vast and irreconcilable social forces fiercely disputed for ascendancy and control; when a heavy curse rested upon our very soil, defying alike the wisdom and the virtue of the people to remove it; when our professions were loudly mocked by our practice and our name was a reproach and a by word to a mocking earth; when our good ship of state, freighted with the best hopes of the oppressed of all nations, was furiously hurled against the hard and flinty rocks of derision, and every cord, bolt, beam and bend in her body quivered beneath the shock, there was some apology for doubt and despair. But that day has happily passed away. The storm has been weathered, and portents are nearly all in our favor.

There are clouds, wind, smoke and dust and noise, over head and around, and there always will be; but no genuine thunder, with destructive bolt, menaces from any quarter of the sky.

The real trouble with us was never our system or form of Government, or the principles underlying it; but the peculiar composition of our people, the relations existing between them and the compromising spirit which controlled the ruling power of the country.

We have for along time hesitated to adopt and may yet refuse to adopt, and carry out, the only principle which can solve that difficulty and give peace, strength and security to the Republic, and that is the principle of absolute equality.

We are a country of all extremes—, ends and opposites; the most conspicuous example of composite nationality in the world. Our people defy all the ethnological and logical classifications. In races we range all the way from black to white, with intermediate shades which, as in the apocalyptic vision, no man can name a number.

In regard to creeds and faiths, the condition is no better, and no worse. Differences both as to race and to religion are evidently more likely to increase than to diminish.

We stand between the populous shores of two great oceans. Our land is capable of supporting one fifth of all the globe. Here, labor is abundant and here labor is better remunerated than any where else. All moral, social and geographical causes, conspire to bring to us the peoples of all other over populated countries.

Europe and Africa are already here, and the Indian was here before either. He stands today between the two extremes of black and white, too proud to claim fraternity with either, and yet too weak to withstand the power of either. Heretofore the policy of our government has been governed by race pride, rather than by wisdom. Until recently, neither the Indian nor the negro has been treated as a part of the body politic. No attempt has been made to inspire either with a sentiment of patriotism, but the hearts of both races have been diligently sown with the dangerous seeds of discontent and hatred.

The policy of keeping the Indians to themselves, has kept the tomahawk and scalping knife busy upon our borders, and has cost us largely in blood and treasure. Our treatment of the negro has slacked humanity, and filled the country with agitation and ill-feeling and brought the nation to the verge of ruin.

Before the relations of these two races are satisfactorily settled, and in spite of all opposition, a new race is making its appearance within our borders, and claiming attention. It is estimated that not less than one hundred thousand Chinamen, are now within the limits of the United States. Several years ago every vessel, large or small, of steam or sail, bound to our Pacific coast and hailing from the Flowery kingdom, added to the number and strength of this new element of our population.

Men differ widely as to the magnitude of this potential Chinese immigration. The fact that by the late treaty with China, we bind ourselves to receive immigrants from that country only as the subjects of the Emperor, and by the construction, at least, are bound not to [naturalize] them, and the further fact that Chinamen themselves have a superstitious devotion to their country and an aversion to permanent location in any other, contracting even to have their bones carried back, should they die abroad, and from the fact that many have returned to China, and the still more stubborn [fact] that resistance to their coming has increased rather than diminished, it is inferred that we shall never have a large Chinese population in America. This however is not my opinion.

It may be admitted that these reasons, and others, may check and moderate the tide of immigration; but it is absurd to think that they will do more than this. Counting their number now, by the thousands, the time is not remote when they will count them by the millions. The Emperor's hold upon the Chinamen may be strong, but the Chinaman's hold upon himself is stronger.

Treaties against naturalization, like all other treaties, are limited by circumstances. As to the superstitious attachment of the Chinese to China, that, like all other superstitions, will dissolve in the light and heat of truth and experience. The Chinaman may be a bigot, but it does not follow that he will continue to be one, tomorrow. He is a man, and will be very likely to act like a man. He will not be long in finding out that a country which is good enough to live in, is good enough to die in; and that a soil that was good enough to hold his body while alive, will be good enough to hold his bones when he is dead.

Those who doubt a large immigration, should remember that the past furnishes no criterion as a basis of calculation. We live under new and improved conditions of migration, and these conditions are constantly improving. America is no longer an obscure and inaccessible country. Our ships are in every sea, our commerce in every port, our language is heard all around the globe, steam and lightning have revolutionized the whole domain of human thought. Changed all geographical relations, make a day of the present seem equal to a thousand years of the past, and the continent that Columbus only conjectured four centuries ago is now the centre of the world.

I believe that Chinese immigration on a large scale will yet be our irrepressible fact. The spirit of race pride will not always prevail. The reasons for this opinion are obvious; China is a vastly overcrowded country. Her people press against each other like cattle in a rail car. Many live upon the water, and have laid out streets upon the waves. Men, like bees, want elbow room. When the hive is overcrowded, the bees will swarm, and will be likely to take up their abode where they find the best prospect for honey. In matters of this sort, men are very much like bees. Hunger will not be quietly endured, even in the celestial empire, when it is once generally known that there is bread enough and to spare in America. What Satan said of Job is true of the Chinaman, as well as of other men,
 "All that a man hath will he give for his life." They will come here to live where they know the means of living are in abundance.

The same mighty forces which have swept our shores the overflowing populations of Europe; which have reduced the people of Ireland three millions below its normal standard; will operate in a similar manner upon the hungry population of China and other parts of Asia. Home has its charms, and native land has its charms, but hunger, oppression, and destitution, will desolve these charms and send men in search of new countries and new homes.

Not only is there a Chinese motive behind this probable immigration, but there is also an American motive which will play its part, one which will be all the more active and energetic because there is in it an element of pride, of bitterness, and revenge.

Southern gentlemen who led in the late rebellion, have not parted with their convictions at this point, any more than at others. They want to be independent of the negro. They believed in slavery and they believe in it still. They believed in an aristocratic class and they believe in it still, and though they have lost slavery, one element essential to such a class, they still have two important conditions to the reconstruction of that class. They have intelligence and they have land. Of these, the land is the more important. They cling to it with all the tenacity of a cherished superstition. They will neither sell to the negro, nor let the carpet baggers have it in peace, but are determined to hold it for themselves and their children forever. They have not yet learned that when a principle is gone, the incident must go also; that what was wise and proper under slavery, is foolish and mischievous in a state of general liberty; that the old bottles are worthless when the new wine has come; but they have found that land is a doubtful benefit where there are no hands to it.

Hence these gentlemen have turned their attention to the Celestial Empire. They would rather have laborers who will work for nothing; but as they cannot get the negroes on these terms, they want Chinamen who, they hope, will work for next to nothing.

Companies and associations may be formed to promote this Mongolian invasion. The loss of the negro is to gain them, the Chinese; and if the thing works well, abolition, in their opinion, will have proved itself to be another blessing in disguise. To the statesman it will mean Southern independence. To the pulpit it will be the hand of Providence, and bring about the time of the universal dominion of the Christian religion. To all but the Chinaman and the negro, it will mean wealth, ease and luxury.

But alas, for all the selfish inventions and dreams of men! The Chinaman will not long be willing to wear the cast off shoes of the negro, and if he refuses, there will be trouble again. The negro worked and took his pay in religion and the lash. The Chinaman is a different article and will want the cash. He may, like the negro, accept Christianity, but unlike the negro he will not care to pay for it in labor under the lash.

He had the golden rule in substance, five hundred years before the coming of Christ, and has notions of justice that are not to be confused or bewildered by any of our "Cursed be Canaan" religion.

Nevertheless, the experiment will be tried. So far as getting the Chinese into our country is concerned, it will yet be a success. This elephant will be drawn by our Southern brethren, though they will hardly know in the end what to do with him.

Appreciation of the value of Chinamen as laborers will, I apprehend, become general in this country. The North was never indifferent to Southern influence and example, and it will not be so in this instance.

The Chinese in themselves have first rate recommendations. They are industrious, docile, cleanly, frugal; they are dexterious of hand, patient of toil, marvelously gifted in the power of imitation, and have but few wants. Those who have carefully observed their habits in California, say they can subsist upon what would be almost starvation to others.

The conclusion of the whole will be that they will want to come to us, and as we become more liberal, we shall want them to come, and what we want will normally be done.

They will no longer halt upon the shores of California. They will borrow no longer in her exhausted and deserted gold mines where they have gathered wealth from bareness, taking what others left. They will turn their backs not only upon the Celestial Empire, but upon the golden shores of the Pacific, and the wide waste of waters whose majestic waves spoke to them of home and country. They will withdraw their eyes from the glowing west and fix them upon the rising sun. They will cross the mountains, cross the plains, descend our rivers, penetrate to the heart of the country and fix their homes with us forever.

Assuming then that this immigration already has a foothold and will continue for many years to come, we have a new element in our national composition which is likely to exercise a large influence upon the thought and the action of the whole nation.

The old question as to what shall be done with [the] negro will have to give place to the greater question, "what shall be done with the Mongolian" and perhaps we shall see raised one even still greater question, namely, what will the Mongolian do with both the negro and the whites?

Already has the matter taken this shape in California and on the Pacific Coast generally. Already has California assumed a bitterly unfriendly attitude toward the Chinamen. Already has she driven them from her altars of justice. Already has she stamped them as outcasts and handed them over to popular contempt and vulgar jest. Already are they the constant victims of cruel harshness and brutal violence.
Already have our Celtic brothers, never slow to execute the behests of popular prejudice against the weak and defenseless, recognized in the heads of these people, fit targets for their shilalahs. Already, too, are their associations formed in avowed hostility to the Chinese.

In all this there is, of course, nothing strange. Repugnance to the presence and influence of foreigners is an ancient feeling among men. It is peculiar to no particularly race or nation. It is met with not only in the conduct of one nation toward another, but in the conduct of the inhabitants of different parts of the same country, some times of the same city, and even of the same village. "Lands intersected by a narrow frith, abhor each other. Mountains interposed, make enemies of nations." To the Hindoo, every man not twice born, is Mleeka. To the Greek, every man not speaking Greek, is a barbarian. To the Jew, every one not circumcised, is a gentile. To the Mahometan, every man not believing in the prophet, is a kaffe. I need not repeat here the multitude of reproachful epithets expressive of the same sentiment among ourselves. All who are not to the manor born, have been made to feel the lash and sting of these reproachful names.

For this feeling there are many apologies, for there was never yet an error, however flagrant and hurtful, for which some plausible defense could not be framed. Chattel slavery, king craft, priest craft, pious frauds, intolerance, persecution, suicide, assassination, repudiation, and a thousand other errors and crimes, have all had their defenses and apologies.

Prejudice of race and color has been equally upheld. The two best arguments in its defense are, first, the worthlessness of the class against which it was directed; and, second; that he feeling itself is entirely natural.

The way to overcome the first argument is, to work for the elevation of those deemed worthless, and thus make them worthy of regard and they will soon become worthy and not worthless. As to the natural argument it may be said, that nature has many sides. Many things are in a certain sense natural, which are neither wise nor best. It is natural to walk, but shall men therefore refuse to ride? It is natural to ride on horseback, shall men therefore refuse steam and rail? Civilization is itself a constant war upon some forces in nature; shall we therefore abandon civilization and go back to savage life?

Nature has two voices, the one is high, the other low; one is in sweet accord with reason and justice, and the other apparently at war with both. The more men really know of the essential nature of things, and on of the true relation of mankind, the freer they are from prejudices of every kind. The child is afraid of the giant form of his own shadow. This is natural, but he will part with his fears when he is older and wiser. So ignorance is full of prejudice, but it will disappear with enlightenment. But I pass on.

I have said that the Chinese will come, and have given some reasons why we may expect them in very large numbers in no very distant future. Do you ask, if I favor such immigration, I answer I would. Would you have them naturalized, and have them invested with all the rights of American citizenship? I would. Would you allow them to vote? I would. Would you allow them to hold office? I would.

But are there not reasons against all this? Is there not such a law or principle as that of self-preservation? Does not every race owe something to itself? Should it not attend to the dictates of common sense? Should not a superior race protect itself from contact with inferior ones? Are not the white people the owners of this continent? Have they not the right to say, what kind of people shall be allowed to come here and settle? Is there not such a thing as being more generous than wise? In the effort to promote civilization may we not corrupt and destroy what we have? Is it best to take on board more passengers than the ship will carry?

To all of this and more I have one among many answers, together satisfactory to me, though I cannot promise that it will be so to you.

I submit that this question of Chinese immigration should be settled upon higher principles than those of a cold and selfish expediency.

There are such things in the world as human rights. They rest upon no conventional foundation, but are external, universal, and indestructible. Among these, is the right of locomotion; the right of migration; the right which belongs to no particular race, but belongs alike to all and to all alike. It is the right you assert by staying here, and your fathers asserted by coming here. It is this great right that I assert for the Chinese and Japanese, and for all other varieties of men equally with yourselves, now and forever. I know of no rights of race superior to the rights of humanity, and when there is a supposed conflict between human and national rights, it is safe to go to the side of humanity. I have great respect for the blue eyed and light haired races of America. They are a mighty people. In any struggle for the good things of this world they need have no fear. They have no need to doubt that they will get their full share.

But I reject the arrogant and scornful theory by which they would limit migratory rights, or any other essential human rights to themselves, and which would make them the owners of this great continent to the exclusion of all other races of men.

I want a home here not only for the negro, the mulatto and the Latin races; but I want the Asiatic to find a home here in the United States, and feel at home here, both for his sake and for ours. Right wrongs no man. If respect is had to majorities, the fact that only one fifth of the population of the globe is white, the other four fifths are colored, ought to have some weight and influence in disposing of this and similar questions. It would be a sad reflection upon the laws of nature and upon the idea of justice, to say nothing of a common Creator, if four fifths of mankind were deprived of the rights of migration to make room for the one fifth. If the white race may exclude all other races from this continent, it may rightfully do the same in respect to all other lands, islands, capes and continents, and thus have all the world to itself. Thus what would seem to belong to the whole, would become the property only of a part. So much for what is right, now let us see what is wise.

And here I hold that a liberal and brotherly welcome to all who are likely to come to the United states, is the only wise policy which this nation can adopt.

It has been thoughtfully observed, that every nation, owing to its peculiar character and composition, has a definite mission in the world. What that mission is, and what policy is best adapted to assist in its fulfillment, is the business of its people and its statesmen to know, and knowing, to make a noble use of said knowledge.

I need to stop here to name or describe the missions of other and more ancient nationalities. Ours seems plain and unmistakable. Our geographical position, our relation to the outside world, our fundamental principles of Government, world embracing in their scope and character, our vast resources, requiring all manner of labor to develop them, and our already existing composite population, all conspire to one grand end, and that is to make us the make perfect national illustration of the unit and dignity of the human family, that the world has ever seen.

In whatever else other nations may have been great and grand, our greatness and grandeur will be found in the faithful application of the principle of perfect civil equality to the people of all races and of all creeds, and to men of no creeds. We are not only bound to this position by our organic structure and by our revolutionary antecedents, but by the genius of our people. Gathered here, from all quarters of the globe by a common aspiration for rational liberty as against caste, divine right Governments and privileged classes, it would be unwise to be found fighting against ourselves and among ourselves; it would be madness to set up any one race above another, or one religion above another, or proscribe any on account of race color or creed.

The apprehension that we shall be swamped or swallowed up by Mongolian civilization; that the Caucasian race may not be able to hold their own against that vast incoming population, does not seem entitled to much respect. Though they come as the waves come, we shall be stronger if we receive them as friends and give them a reason for loving our country and our institutions. They will find here a deeply rooted, indigenous, growing civilization, augmented by an ever increasing stream of immigration from Europe; and possession is nine points of the law in this case, as well as in others. They will come as strangers, we are at home. They will come to us, not we to them. They will come in their weakness, we shall meet them in our strength. They will come as individuals, we will meet them in multitudes, and with all the advantages of organization. Chinese children are in American schools in San Francisco, none of our children are in Chinese schools, and probably never will be, though in some things they might well teach us valuable lessons.

Contact with these yellow children of The Celestial Empire would convince us that the points of human difference, great as they, upon first sight, seem, are as nothing compared with the points of human agreement. Such contact would remove mountains of prejudice.

It is said that it is not good for man to be alone. This is true not only in the sense in which our woman's rights friends so zealously and wisely teach, but it is true as to nations.

The voice of civilization speaks an unmistakable language against the isolation of families, nations and races, and pleads for composite nationality as essential to her triumphs.

Those races of men which have maintained the most separate and distinct existence for the longest periods of time; which have had the least intercourse with other races of men, are a standing confirmation of the folly of isolation. The very soil of the national mind becomes, in such cases, barren, and can only be resuscitated by assistance from without.

Look at England, whose mighty power is now felt, and for centuries has been felt, all around the world. It is worthy of special remark, that precisely those parts of that proud Island which have received the largest and most diverse populations, are today, the parts most distinguished for industry, enterprise, invention and general enlightenment. In Wales, and in the Highlands of Scotland, the boast is made of their pure blood and that they were never conquered, but no man can contemplate them without wishing they had been conquered.

They are far in the rear of every other part of the English realm in all the comforts and conveniences of life, as well as in mental and physical development. Neither law nor learning descends to us from the mountains of Wales or from the Highlands of Scotland. The ancient Briton whom Julius Caesar would not have a slave, is not to be compared with the round, burly, a[m]plitudinous Englishman in many of the qualities of desirable manhood.

The theory that each race of men has come special faculty, some peculiar gift or quality of mind or heart, needed to the perfection and happiness of the whole is a broad and beneficent theory, and besides its beneficence, has in its support, the voice of experience. Nobody doubts this theory when applied to animals and plants, and no one can show that it is not equally true when applied to races.

All great qualities are never found in any one man or in any one race. The whole of humanity, like the whole of everything else, is ever greater than a part. Men only know themselves by knowing others, and contact is essential to this knowledge. In one race we perceive the predominance of imagination; in another, like Chinese, we remark its total absence.

In one people, we have the reasoning faculty, in another, for music; in another, exists courage; in another, great physical vigor; and so on through the whole list of human qualities. All are needed to temper, modify, round and complete.

Not the least among the arguments whose consideration should dispose to welcome among us the peoples of all countries, nationalities and color, is the fact that all races and varieties of men are improvable. This is the grand distinguishing attribute of humanity and separates man from all other animals. If it could be shown that any particular race of men are literally incapable of improvement, we might hesitate to welcome them here. But no such men are anywhere to be found, and if there were, it is not likely that they would ever trouble us with their presence.

The fact that the Chinese and other nations desire to come and do come, is a proof of their capacity for improvement and of their fitness to come.

We should take council of both nature and art in the consideration of this question. When the architect intends a grand structure, he makes the foundation broad and strong. We should imitate this prudence in laying the foundation of the future Republic. There is a law of harmony in departments of nature. The oak is in the acorn. The career and destiny of individual men are enfolded in the elements of which they are composed. The same is true of a nation. It will be something or it will be nothing. It will be great, or it will be small, according to its own essential qualities. As these are rich and varied, or poor and simple, slender and feeble, broad and strong, so will be the life and destiny of the nation itself.

The stream cannot rise higher than its source. The ship cannot sail faster than the wind. The flight of the arrow depends upon the strength and elasticity of the bow; and as with these, so with a nation.

If we would reach a degree of civilization higher and grander than any yet attained, we should welcome to our ample continent all nations, kindreds [sic] tongues and peoples; and as fast as they learn our language and comprehend the duties of citizenship, we should incorporate them into the American body politic. The outspread wings of the American eagle are broad enough to shelter all who are likely to come.

As a matter of selfish policy, leaving right and humanity out of the question, we cannot wisely pursue any other course. Other Governments mainly depend for security upon the sword; our depends mainly upon the friendship of its people. In all matters,—in time of peace, in time of war, and at all times,—it makes its appeal to all the people, and to all classes of the people. Its strength lies in their friendship and cheerful support in every time of need, and that policy is a mad one which would reduce the number of its friends by excluding those who would come, or by alienating those who are already here.

Our Republic is itself a strong argument in favor of composite nationality. It is no disparagement to Americans of English descent, to affirm that much of the wealth, leisure, culture, refinement and civilization of the country are due to the arm of the negro and the muscle of the Irishman. Without these and the wealth created by their sturdy toil, English civilization had still lingered this side of the Alleghanies [sic], and the wolf still be howling on their summits.

To no class of our population are we more indebted to valuable qualities of head, heart and hand than the German. Say what we will of their lager, their smoke and their metaphysics they have brought to us a fresh, vigorous and child-like nature; a boundless facility in the acquisition of knowledge; a subtle and far reaching intellect, and a fearless love of truth. Though remarkable for patient and laborious thought the true German is a joyous child of freedom, fond of manly sports, a lover of music, and a happy man generally. Though he never forgets that he is a German, he never fails to remember that he is an American.

A Frenchman comes here to make money, and that is about all that need be said of him. He is only a Frenchman. He neither learns our language nor loves our country. His hand is on our pocket and his eye on Paris. He gets what he wants and like a sensible Frenchman, returns to France to spend it.

Now let me answer briefly some objections to the general scope of my arguments. I am told that science is against me; that races are not all of one origin, and that the unity theory of human origin has been exploded. I admit that this is a question that has two sides. It is impossible to trace the threads of human history sufficiently near their starting point to know much about the origin of races.

In disposing of this question whether we shall welcome or repel immigration from China, Japan, or elsewhere, we may leave the differences among the theological doctors to be settled by themselves.

Whether man originated at one time and one or another place; whether there was one Adam or five, or five hundred, does not affect the question.

The grand right of migration and the great wisdom of incorporating foreign elements into our body politic, are founded not upon any genealogical or archeological theory, however learned, but upon the broad fact of a common human nature.

Man is man, the world over. This fact is affirmed and admitted in any effort to deny it. The sentiments we exhibit, whether love or hate, confidence or fear, respect or contempt, will always imply a like humanity.

A smile or a tear has not nationality; joy and sorrow speak alike to all nations, and they, above all the confusion of tongues, proclaim the brotherhood of man.

It is objected to the Chinaman that he is secretive and treacherous, and will not tell the truth when he thinks it for his interest to tell a lie.

There may be truth in all this; it sounds very much like the account of man's heart given in the creeds. If he will not tell the truth except when it is for his interest to do so, let us make it for this interest to tell the truth We can do it by applying to him the same principle of justice that we apply ourselves.

But I doubt if the Chinese are more untruthful than other people. At this point I have one certain test,—mankind are not held together by lies. Trust is the foundation of society. Where there is no truth, there can be no trust, and where there is no trust there can be no society. Where there is society, there is trust, and where there is trust, there is something upon which it is supported. Now a people who have confided in each other for five thousand years; who have extended their empire in all direction till it embraces on e fifth of the population of the glove; who hold important commercial relations with all nations; who are now entering into treaty stipulations with ourselves, and with all the great European powers, cannot be a nation of cheats and liars, but must have some respect for veracity. The very existence of China for so long a period, and her progress in civilization, are proofs of her truthfulness. But it is said that the Chinese is a heathen, and that he will introduce his heathen rights and superstitions here. This is the last objection which should come from those who profess the all conquering power of the Christian religion. If that religion cannot stand contact with the Chinese, religion or no religion, so much the worse for those who have adopted it. It is the Chinaman, not the Christian, who should be alarmed for his faith. He exposes that faith to great dangers by exposing it to the freer air of America. But shall we send missionaries to the heathen and yet deny the heathen the right to come to us? I think that a few honest believers in the teachings of Confucius would be well employed in expounding his doctrines among us.

The next objection to the Chinese is that he cannot be induced to swear by the Bible. This is to me one of his best recommendations. The American people will swear by anything in the heavens above or in the earth beneath. We are a nation of swearers. We swear by a book whose most authoritative command is to swear not at all.

It is not of so much importance what a man swears by, as what he swears to, and if the Chinaman is so true to his convictions that he cannot be tempted or even coerced into so popular a custom as swearing by the Bible, he gives good evidence of his integrity and his veracity.

Let the Chinaman come; he will help to augment the national wealth. He will help to develop our boundless resources; he will help to pay off our national debt. He will help to lighten the burden of national taxation. He will give us the benefit of his skill as a manufacturer and tiller of the soil, in which he is unsurpassed.

Even the matter of religious liberty, which has cost the world more tears, more blood and more agony, than any other interest, will be helped by his presence. I know of no church, however tolerant; of no priesthood, however enlightened, which could be safely trusted with the tremendous power which universal conformity would confer.

We should welcome all men of every shade of religious opinion, as among the best means of checking the arrogance and intolerance which are the almost inevitable concomitants of general conformity. Religious liberty always flourishes best amid the clash and competition of rival religious creeds.

To the minds of superficial men, the fusion of different races has already brought disaster and ruin upon the country. The poor negro has been charged with all our woes. In the haste of these men they forgot that our trouble was not ethnographical, but moral; that it was not a difference of complexion, but a difference of conviction. It was not the Ethiopian as a man, but the Ethiopian as a slave and a covetted [sic] article of merchandise, that gave us trouble.

I close these remarks as I began. If our action shall be in accordance with the principles of justice, liberty, and perfect human equality, no eloquence can adequately portray the greatness and grandeur of the future of the Republic.

We shall spread the network of our science and civilization over all who seek their shelter whether from Asia, Africa, or the Isles of the sea. We shall mold them all, each after his kind, into Americans; Indian and Celt; negro and Saxon; Latin and Teuton; Mongolian and Caucasian; Jew and Gentile; all shall here bow to the same law, speak the same language, support the same Government, enjoy the same liberty, vibrate with the same national enthusiasm, and seek the same national ends.[22]

---

[22] Douglass Papers, Library of Congress, microfilm reel 14.

Analysis of:

Frederick Douglass has never been given his proper due by this country and indeed from the entire world, but I have incomplete knowledge; perhaps there is some province in Mainland China who annually celebrates the bravery and audacity of a recently freed black man to stand up for their rights in America. I know factually that 98% of African-Americans no nothing of this bold accomplishment and to even a less degree of white Americans unless they have academic training in American history. I can't even venture a number for Asian Americans who have knowledge of this legacy and based on the superiority responses we generally hear about, it would seem that Asians feel no debt of gratitude to African-Americans, but let's not accept that as fact. In the 2012 re-election of President Barack Obama, the first African-American elected to the office, it has been reported that upwards of 67% of Asian-Americans voted for him. The student of truth in politics must be very careful to analyze the data, because a large portion of it may have been deliberately skewed.

In the society that comprises a nation, Douglass spoke that they are aggregations of molded into a mighty unit; when they accept and appreciate the power of diversity to create an uncommon juggernaut. It requires a release of selfish aims to elevate ourselves from barbarism in pursuit of loftier and better goals. Douglass dared to ask the fundamental question as to if we are better or worse off for being an amalgamation of races and peoples; does it strengthen us or make us weaker? America he said was in its adolescents of development, with opportunity and energy unequaled at its present time, while other nations suffer the geriatric pain long on experience, but have left many milestones in the evolution of human rights unturned. It is for this cause, he argues that this great nation was born and this is her destiny.

Declaration of Sentiments and Resolutions

Woman's Rights Convention, Held at Seneca Falls, 19-20 July 1848

When, in the course of human events, it becomes necessary for one portion of the family of man to assume among the people of the earth a position different from that which they have hitherto occupied, but one to which the laws of nature and of nature's God entitle them, a decent respect to the opinions of mankind requires that they should declare the causes that impel them to such a course.

We hold these truths to be self-evident: that all men and women are created equal; that they are endowed by their Creator with certain inalienable rights; that among these are life, liberty, and the pursuit of happiness; that to secure these rights governments are instituted, deriving their just powers from the consent of the governed. Whenever any form of Government becomes destructive of these ends, it is the right of those who suffer from it to refuse allegiance to it, and to insist upon the institution of a new government, laying its foundation on such principles, and organizing its powers in such form as to them shall seem most likely to effect their safety and happiness. Prudence, indeed, will dictate that governments long established should not be changed for light and transient causes; and accordingly, all experience hath shown that mankind are more disposed to suffer, while evils are sufferable, than to right themselves by abolishing the forms to which they are accustomed. But when a long train of abuses and usurpations, pursuing invariably the same object, evinces a design to reduce them under absolute despotism, it is their duty to throw off such government, and to provide new guards for their future security. Such has been the patient sufferance of the women under this government, and such is now the necessity which constrains them to demand the equal station to which they are entitled.

The history of mankind is a history of repeated injuries and usurpations on the part of man toward woman, having in direct object the establishment of an absolute tyranny over her. To prove this, let facts be submitted to a candid world.

He has never permitted her to exercise her inalienable right to the elective franchise.

He has compelled her to submit to laws, in the formation of which she had no voice.

He has withheld from her rights which are given to the most ignorant and degraded men—both natives and foreigners.

Having deprived her of this first right of a citizen, the elective franchise, thereby leaving her without representation in the halls of legislation, he has oppressed her on all sides.

He has made her, if married, in the eye of the law, civilly dead.[4]

He has taken from her all right in property, even to the wages she earns.[5]

He has made her, morally, an irresponsible being, as she can commit many crimes with impunity, provided they be done in the presence of her husband. In the covenant of marriage, she is compelled to promise obedience to her husband, he becoming, to all intents and purposes, her master—the law giving him power to deprive her of her liberty, and to administer chastisement.

He has so framed the laws of divorce, as to what shall be the proper causes of divorce; in case of separation, to whom the guardianship of the children shall be given; as to be wholly regardless of the happiness of women—the law, in all cases, going upon the false supposition of the supremacy of man, and giving all power into his hands.

After depriving her of all rights as a married woman, if single and the owner of property, he has taxed her to support a government which recognizes her only when her property can be made profitable to it.

He has monopolized nearly all the profitable employments, and from those she is permitted to follow, she receives but a scanty remuneration.

He closes against her all the avenues to wealth and distinction, which he considers most honorable to himself. As a teacher of theology, medicine, or law, she is not known.

He has denied her the facilities for obtaining a thorough education—all colleges being closed against her.[6]

He allows her in Church as well as State, but a subordinate position, claiming Apostolic authority for her exclusion from the ministry, and, with some exceptions, from any public participation in the affairs of the Church.

He has created a false public sentiment, by giving to the world a different code of morals for men and women, by which moral delinquencies which exclude women from society, are not only tolerated but deemed of little account in man.

He has usurped the prerogative of Jehovah himself, claiming it as his right to assign for her a sphere of action, when that belongs to her conscience and her God.

He has endeavored, in every way that he could to destroy her confidence in her own powers, to lessen her self-respect, and to make her willing to lead a dependent and abject life.

Now, in view of this entire disfranchisement of one-half the people of this country, their social and religious degradation,—in view of the unjust laws above mentioned, and because women do feel themselves aggrieved, oppressed, and fraudulently deprived of their most sacred rights, we insist that they have immediate admission to all the rights and privileges which belong to them as citizens of these United States.

In entering upon the great work before us, we anticipate no small amount of misconception, misrepresentation, and ridicule; but we shall use every instrumentality within our power to effect our object. We shall employ agents, circulate tracts, petition the State and national Legislatures, and endeavor to enlist the pulpit and the press in our behalf. We hope this Convention will be followed by a series of Conventions, embracing every part of the country.

Firmly relying upon the final triumph of the Right and the True, we do this day affix our signatures to this declaration.

At the appointed hour the meeting convened. The minutes having been read, the resolutions of the day before were read and taken up separately. Some, from their self-evident truth, elicited but little remark; others, after some criticism, much debate, and some slight alterations, were finally passed by a large majority.

[At an evening session] Lucretia Mott offered and spoke to the following resolution:

Resolved, That the speedy success of our cause depends upon the zealous and untiring efforts of both men and women, for the overthrow of the monopoly of the pulpit, and for the securing to woman an equal participation with men in the various trades, professions and commerce.

The Resolution was adopted.[23]

---

[23] *Report of the Woman's Rights Convention, Held at Seneca Falls, N.Y., July 19th and 20th, 1848* (Rochester, 1848). Prepared for the *Selected Papers of Elizabeth Cady Stanton and Susan B. Anthony*, vol. 1, *In the School of Anti-Slavery, 1840 to 1866*, ed. Ann D. Gordon (New Brunswick, N.J., 1997). ©Rutgers, The State University of New Jersey.

Analysis: The Progressive Party Platform (1912)[24]

The Progressive Party formulated its doctrine by a group of activists; female, labor reformers and social scientists, for what is arguably the blueprint for a democratic welfare state or as party candidate, Theodore Roosevelt describes it; the " most important document" since the end of the Civil War. Depending on which side of the political argument you find yourself in agreement, the policies, promises and prognostications all possess a small segment of clairvoyance, both then and now, with its share of accomplishment and disappointment. Many of Roosevelt's views in his New Nationalism were prescience in their long term vision with regards to taxes, big corporations and federal regulation, however given the ever changing cycle of political leadership, future politicians would refute and seek to overturn progressive momentum.

The platform starts by appealing to American conscience, a bold and broad stroke of paradoxes and political puffing. It paraphrases sections of the Declaration of Independence and cites America's most well-known progenitors of justice and equality, Jefferson and Lincoln, no doubt to wake up that conscience referenced in its preamble. Like the Constitution and the Declaration, the Progressive Party Platform makes sweeping generalities of equality of inclusion that historically America had yet to honor.

In the section titled 'The Old Parties', the document castigates the former leadership in both style and deed. As a solution it lays the foundation for the formation of a new party, more responsive to the will and needs of the people, uncorrupted by self and special interests and unafraid to take on

---

[24] Source Donald B. Johnson, comp., National Party Platforms (Urbana, Ill., 1978), Vol. 1, pp. 175-179
"The Progressive Party Platform.*"* *Voices of Freedom*. Ed. Eric Foner. New York * London: W.W. Norton & Company, 2nd Vol, 3rd Ed, 2011. 98 – 106. Print

the enormous tasks set before it. To seal this commitment, the Progressive Party makes a statement of covenant with the people.

Promising to be more representative of the people, it pledges to alter the law when and where necessary to restore the rights that the American people will want to respect and preserve. It is here that the platform suggests specifics:

- Direct primaries for both state and national offices.

- Preferential primaries for the office of the President.

- Direct election of U.S. Senators.

- The use of referendum, initiative and recall.

The Progressive Party Platform espouses the usage of amending the Constitution as need be, to streamline and bring unity to those policies that are skewed in individual states. It specifically cites the Democratic Parties in Baltimore advocating on behalf of the states' rights of Maryland, a position the Progressive Party finds arcane and void of political understanding.

On the matters of women's suffrage the Progressives succinctly pledge to secure enfranchisement for women. (Again somewhat paradoxically not drawing distinction based on race or ethnicity leaving a gapping generality to be argued in some future venue.)

An important heading to address the issues long gone neglected were described *as Social and Industrial Strength.* Topics like the abuse of employees working hours, conditions in the workplace, child labor, minimum wage etc. were placed under this broad umbrella, with forethought to include elevation by the establishment of trade schools to further enhance quality and quantity of a future labor force.

Some of these proposals were the impetus for future regulation, legislation and the creation of several new bureaucratic agencies like the Department of Labor, Health and Human Services, the Environmental Protection Agency, Department of Agriculture, Occupation, Safety and Health Administration to name a few.

In business, the focus was the introduction of legislation to create the Interstate Commerce Commission, which would be given broad oversight of the operation and expansions of corporations to avoid the creation of monopolies and entities that have the power to manipulate markets at the expense of the workers and the consumers.

The Progressive Platform in my estimation may have been one of the most far reaching and most well planned proposals to have been introduced to the public and government since the Constitution and the Bill of Rights. There is no single set of proposals produced by Americans to address the problems and situations of a burgeoning growing industrial complex like the United States of America as comprehensive and specific as the Progressive Party Platform and perhaps the time has come to assess the outcomes.

The Internet and Cable Television: Enter the Information Age

"Life is really simple, but we insist on making it complicated."

Confucius

The biological nature of mankind has many facets, one of which is the quest to expand and improve on ways to communicate information. In the Bible, there was the Tower of Babel, where man in his zeal to please and communicate directly with God, joined with people under a common language to build a tower high into the heavens. God was not pleased! He purposely confused their tongues separating people on the basis of language, wherein they each scattered to his or her own region. Has electronic communication technology become the new Tower of Babel?

In politics the person with the most exposure, the candidate whose name is easily recognizable and has made for themselves an indelible icon into the mind's eye of the voter, is generally likely the one to be most remembered when the curtain of the voting booth closes on Election Day. Thanks to the social media of our present era, a person with a modest financial beginning can catapult him or herself into the media spotlight, almost for free, and then begin to spin the web of fundraising for a campaign, because exposure is a game of saturation. What used to take days, months even years of stumping can be accomplished in seconds over the internet. In the vernacular of the day; if something goes viral then you, then the hits, our amount of times your product is viewed increases exponentially.

Almost if not all subject and opinion can be falsely corroborated and find common incongruence on the World Wide Web. There is someone within the reaches of the internet who will agree with the most innocuous, idiotic, asinine opinion, unsubstantiated by fact and void of logic or scientific verification, but has uncovered some like-minded fool(s) that will hail it as the discovery of the Holy Grail. The strange behavior of politicians in the present age perhaps can partially be attributed to this marvel of technological science, because there are those that surely stay at wake at night to conjure up these bizarre positions in the guise of representing the people. Currently in Washington D.C. there is an argument over the extension of the debt ceiling. Some would have us believe that the best way to get the government, not the taxpayers, into line is to deny the extension forcing millions of Americans out of work and crippling social services almost to the point of social anarchy. This is about as bright as sending a fireman up a ladder to fight a fire, then pulling it out from under him or her when they reach the fire. Two immediate things are bound to happen; you won't put out the fire and the method you chose to fight the problem is bound to get someone hurt. Thirdly, you stand the risk of destroying the thing you were trying to protect and preserve beyond repair. The examples of incompetence are legion and it may take social and political scientists decades to make a direct connection of the behavior of politicians with the internet, but I don't have the time to wait and I have drawn some conclusions. Unscientific though they may be, the level of lunacy in politics has escalated every time we (Americans) introduce a new median to deliver a message or feed our narcissism.

Television produced a similar result and you can trace for yourself through historical footage how the early users of television were cautious and stiff, but as they became more comfortable with it, they began to loosen up and start competing for exposure. Once a politico discovered that a man in a clown suit is more memorable and talked about then a guy standing erect in Brooks Brother's suit, the media circus was off to the races. (I wonder why God didn't smite that Babel in its infancy; maybe he/she does have a sense of humor!) We can even go farther back in time to the days of radio, when the early users talked in relatively normal speech, though somewhat loudly to the later era where voices were augmented, vocal chords stretched and falsetto's were formed to capture an audience abducted by audiles where the cleverest of speech had the ability to paint word pictures that had the power to persuade.

The internet is a beast all unto itself! Politicians try to use it, manipulate it, hire web designers, use it for fundraising, leaks to media and defamation of enemies. They can colorize, airbrush, photo shop images, and plagiarize in the instance of hitting save or send. Mediums such as Facebook, Twitter and Instagram have made babbling idiots from many men and women who wished that they had not hit send. Confusion, stupidity, boredom or shear narcissism. It boggles the mind! More gets invented before we have mastered the last. Inject politics into this digital media maze and you can start wars. Imagine Lincoln or Jefferson with the power of such communication; aliens will leave us alone for another million millenniums.

Money and Politics

"In a country well governed, poverty is something to be ashamed of. In a country badly governed, wealth is something to be ashamed of."

Confucius

McCutcheon et al. v. Federal Election Commission

On April 2, 2014, the Supreme Court issued a 5-4 ruling that the 1971 FECA's aggregate limits restricting how much money a donor may contribute in total to all candidates or committees violated the First Amendment. The controlling opinion was written by Chief Justice Roberts, and joined by Justices Scalia, Alito and Kennedy; Justice Thomas concurred in the judgment but wrote separately to argue that *all* limits on contributions were unconstitutional. Justice Breyer filed a dissenting opinion, joined by Justices Ginsburg, Kagan and Sotomayor.

In my book titled, "Lazarus Man, Return to the Howard Universe", I stated that hypothetically or expressed as a parable: Two merchants were driving their pigs to market. The first merchant owns ten pigs and the second has three. Which merchant deserves or demands the right of way on the road?

The point is, not only is to whom much is given, much is required, but also to whom is favored by wealth demands a prominent seat in the temple.

Money is said to be the mother's milk of politics, in deed, actions and easily verifiable evidence, it has proven to be so. Regionally, on the east and west coasts a person cannot mount the most localized campaign without money. Within the Midwest and in very rural areas name recognition may be enough to wage a successful attempt in running for public office. Family status, local business ownership and the reputation of just being the local rabble rouser may be sufficient to get a person elected, but in the heavily urban areas, money is the bread cast on the waters of politics that establishes a person's hierarchy in garnering favor with the electorate and there is substitute.

What exactly can money purchase to win elections? In the most basic and elemental level of campaigning one needs to be able to purchase a venue, staff and creative persons to get an audience capable of raising funds. In essence this means that in order to get money one must spend large amounts of amounts to support a candidate. Like bees to honey, one must first cultivate a flower. Through market research, a person must grow a flower unique in capturing the flavors and aroma which attracts the bees; not just any bee but one that is capable of producing nectar. Simultaneously your opponent has planted his/her own garden to steal the largesse and product of the same donors you wish so desperately to attract. When a person spends money an unspoken quid pro quo is established, a relationship that is as much silent as it is deadly. Not only deadly but highly regressive always reminding the benefactor that the piper is due his pay. Unfortunately this a human condition that reaches far beyond the political arena;

I have friends who remind me of when they bought me a drink, a hamburger or a soda at the local drug store many eons ago and they still demand consideration for what should have otherwise been a gesture so innocuous as sharing the air that we breathe.

Campaign events are costly and depending on the venue can be more expensive than a daughter's wedding. The saddest part of the whole experience is that the majority of this seed money rarely yields edible fruit.

So then how does one quantify or justify this expensive gamble. The candidate can envision oneself on the victor's podium, one can imagine with the hubris endowed in all politicians of doing some great and magnanimous thing that will serve the electorate and edify one's self into the annals of political greatness, while forgetting that the devil will demand his due. The cost to family, friends and self will leave gapping wounds that will bleed continuously and the blood cannot be staunched by an insincere smile and promises left unpaid.

Money, the root of all evil, will be the veins and arteries that carry the message so craftily constructed to add confusion and subterfuge in the arts of politics. Many a man and woman will bow on bended knee, be they religious, atheist or agnostic and beg to achieve some purpose that will vindicate their whoredom. It will be money that catapults one to success and money which will exact a price on one's soul.

Absurd Promises by Politicians

"Silence is a true friend who never betrays."

Confucius

We all have access to the vain words and deeds of politicians. They are too voluminous for this abridged volume of regurgitation however let us examine:

"**Democracy** is hypocrisy without limitation."[25]

Iskander Mirza: Major-General **Sahibzada Sayyid Iskander Ali Mirza**, CIE, OBE English IPA: ɪskɑndær əɪi: mi(ə)ɹzə (Urdu: اسکندر مرزا ;اسکندر مرزا; Bengali: ইস্কান্দার মীর্জা; 13 November 1898 – 12 November 1969), was the first President of Pakistan, serving from 1956 until being forced out from the presidency in 1958.[1] Prior to that, Mirza was the last Governor-General of Pakistan from 1955 until 1956.[1] A great-grandson of the last Nawab of Bengal Mir Jafar,[2] Mirza was the first president of Pakistan and a retired career army officer, having reached the higher rank of major-general in Pakistan Army.[26]

"**Hypocrisy** in anything whatever may deceive the cleverest and most penetrating man, but the least wide-awake of children recognizes it, and is revolted by it, however ingeniously it may be disguised."[27]

Leo Tolstoy: Count Lev Nikolayevich Tolstoy, also known as Leo Tolstoy, was a Russian writer who primarily wrote novels and short stories. Tolstoy was a master of realistic fiction and is widely considered one of the world's greatest novelists.[28]

"Every man alone is sincere. At the entrance of a second person, hypocrisy begins."

RALPH WALDO EMERSON[29], "Friendship," *Essays*

"The people who make wars, the people who reduce their fellows to slavery, the people who kill and torture and tell lies in the name of their sacred causes, the really evil people in a word—these are never the publicans and the sinners. No, they're the virtuous, respectable men, who have the finest feelings, the best brains, the noblest ideals."[30]

ALDOUS HUXLEY, *After Many a Summer Dies the Swan*

"I think that generally one of the things that—one of the things that I sort of feel like is the meta issue in the type of political commentary that I do is that nobody really cares about hypocrisy—everybody expects hypocrisy from politicians. And so, you tell a politician they are being a hypocrite, and they say, oh, you have such a nasty tune, stop saying those rude things, because they don't care about the substance of it."[31]

RACHEL MADDOW, *The Rachel Maddow Show*, Jul. 5, 2011

"Outside of the killings, Washington has one of the lowest crime rates in the country." —Marion Barry, former mayor of Washington, D.C.[32]

"Well, I learned a lot....I went down to (Latin America) to find out from them and (learn) their views. You'd be surprised. They're all individual countries" — Ronald Reagan[33]

28

[29] "Friendship," *Essays* (Notable Quotes)
[30] After Many a Summer Dies the Swan (Notable Quotes)
[31] *The Rachel Maddow Show*, Jul. 5, 2011
[32] Marion Barry ©2013 About.com. All rights reserved.
[33] Ronal Reagan ©2013 About.com. All rights reserved.

"It is the duty of every citizen according to his best capacities
to give validity to his convictions in political affairs."[34]

Albert Einstein (1879 - 1955), *'Treasury for the Free World,' 1946*

"Crime does not pay ... as well as politics."[35]

Alfred E. Newman

"Politics has never been for the thin-skinned or the faint of
heart, and if you enter the arena , you should expect to get
roughed up. Moreover, Democracy in a nation of more than
300 million people is inherently difficult."[36]

Barack Obama (1961 -), *University of Michigan
Commencement, 2010*

---

[34] Albert Einstein **(1879 - 1955)**, *'Treasury for the Free World,' 1946*

[35] Alfred E. Newman

[36] Barack Obama **(1961 -)**, *University of Michigan Commencement, 2010*

Epilogue

"Knowledge is merely brilliance in organization of ideas and not wisdom. The truly wise person goes beyond knowledge."

Confucius

Pragmatism or Principle: Expedience for Political Ideology

When a candidate hears the call to public service, the next step in planning must be the development of a platform on which to run. It would seem to be self-evident that the candidate has identified a void that needs to be filled and vulnerability in the likely opponents' policies. Exploratory analysis of everything within the district i.e. demographics, voting patterns, and most important the constituent issues must be assessed. Framing of the campaign strategy should be the next logical step based on the results of the collected data. This is in essence the business plan that the candidate uses to sell his/her ability to win campaign donors. The question is; why political ideology and party philosophy replaced the altruism of a candidate to do what is best for the community and address the needs of the majority of its constituents?

Looking back over the Republican primary debates (2011), one can only conclude that the recent group of candidates had substituted their individual principle over pragmatism or stood on principle when pragmatism would have been more expedient.

Most if not all of the candidates answered questions on policy by saying categorically that they would cut several institutions and/or existing legislation in appeasement to political factions with deep pockets and make claim to having large and active bases. They hung their hats on words and phrases like conservatism, right wing, big government, deficit spending and expanding debt as the new moral suasion representative of principle, but lacking pragmatism to win elections. One candidate, Governor Rick Perry of Texas, stood on the debate platform and within a single breath said that if elected he would dissolve the Departments of Education, Commerce and the third one he couldn't remember (Energy) in the opening days of his administration. The three agencies combined represented about 15,000 employees in the Metropolitan Washington region and another number that could exceed 25,000 nationwide; not to mention the ancillary support organizations, small business contractors, grant recipients and citizens who benefit from those agencies; principle or pragmatism? In an effort to curry favor with conservatives some of the other candidates stated how punitive their policies would be on immigration, alienating a burgeoning politically active group. Not satisfied with the forays already made to the conservative base, they attacked healthcare reform and instead of suggesting pragmatic solutions to the problems of Medicare, they sought to obscure the present program in order to engender fear. The most curious of all positions that they propositioned was to heavy handedly espouse control of the moral, intellectual and physical lives of women, an invaluable and highly consistent group of voters.

Expedience by the advancement of ideology is the death Nell of pragmatism when a person is trying to get elected. When a candidate is running for office, they would do wise to say on programs or institutions that are already implemented that they will initiate exploratory committees and commissions to improve efficiency and determine their continued efficacy to meet the needs of the people.

To allay fears, especially in a troubled economy, they would need to say that before slashing or terminating a program, alternative applications and/or outsourcing of those services will precede any draconian action. When the administration of George W. Bush took office in 2001 from his predecessor, Bill Clinton, he jokingly, I hoped at the time, said that he would overturn, overhaul or remove everything done by the previous President. That was a bold ideological move, full of the principles that he ran on during the election, which was a great sound bite to his base, but it was pragmatically illogical, or for a lack of a better phrase, 'galactically' stupid. There is not one person who is reading this article who is not aware of where that has gotten us.

Back in the bad old days, before all of the new technology and 24 hour cable, a politician could go into one venue and talk mountain hillbilly, throw in a little Spanish or Italian to those audiences, speak a few Ebonics phrases when addressing a black audience and shout 'hallelujahs' to Evangelicals without one group ever completely finding out exactly what was said to the other. That is no longer true. Now because the entire world can read, see and hear exactly what a candidate is saying almost instantaneously, then the true position and the group the candidate most needs or fears most is monitoring non-stop for consistency. If a candidate maintains his/her own personal integrity, opinion and beliefs and shares them on the campaign trail without a clear understanding or appreciation for the majority opinion, he/she places themselves in severe risk of losing the election, ultimately it is the individual vote that will prevail. It has become pragmatic to remain deliberately vague, with as few promises as possible. Candidates are caught in a classic 'Catch 22', trying to appeal to the electorate and appeasing a well-funded base. If you accept the adage that 'money talks', then the candidate is torn between acquiescing to the will of the single interest donors versus the collective interests of the majority. As a result, and here lies the paradox, policy is shaped more by immediate pragmatism and less on principle.

This is the dynamic quality of politics and is the core reason why elected government must be continually stimulated by constituents. Unfortunately for us all, principles can be bought, but there is no substitute for pragmatism.

PERMISSIONS

Text is available under the Creative Commons Attribution-ShareAlike License; additional terms may apply. By using this site, you agree to the Terms of Use and Privacy Policy. Wikipedia® is a registered trademark of the Wikimedia Foundation, Inc., a non-profit organization.

- **Read and Print** our articles and other media free of charge.
- **Share and Reuse** our articles and other media under free and open licenses.
- **Contribute To and Edit** our various sites or Projects.

www.ingramcontent.com/pod-product-compliance
Lightning Source LLC
Chambersburg PA
CBHW070206290526
45789CB00002B/931